VIRTUAL
PRESENTATIONS
THAT **WORK**

JOEL GENDELMAN, ED.D.

New York   Chicago   San Francisco
Lisbon   London   Madrid   Mexico City   Milan
New Delhi   San Juan   Seoul   Singapore
Sydney   Toronto

1 2 3 4 5 6 7 8 9 0 WFR/WFR 1 5 4 3 2 1 0

ISBN: 978-0-07-173936-8
MHID: 0-07-173936-X

This publication is designed to provide accurate and authoritative information in regard to the subject matter covered. It is sold with the understanding that the publisher is not engaged in rendering legal, accounting, or other professional service. If legal advice or other expert assistance is required, the services of a competent professional person should be sought.

—From a declaration of principles jointly adopted by a committee of the American Bar Association and a committee of publishers

McGraw-Hill books are available at special quantity discounts to use as premiums and sales promotions, or for use in corporate training programs. To contact a representative please visit the Contact Us pages at www.mhprofessional.com.

CONTENTS

INTRODUCTION

Nothing happens unless first we dream.

—Carl Sandburg

Every company is seeking inexpensive ways to operate faster, reduce expenses, and reach out to a continuously widening global marketplace. So how do managers and executives accomplish that without decreasing quality, customer satisfaction, and employee morale? More and more, they are relying upon virtual presentations, which have the added benefits of being more convenient for both the speaker and the audience. On a busy day, the number of virtual presentations and meetings hosted by a single service provider may exceed 100,000. That is a lot of meetings!

Regrettably, though, these presentations tend to be even more boring (and less effective) than their face-to-face counterparts.

Most new technologies follow a life cycle. At first, they simply emulate older technologies, although hopefully a bit faster and cheaper. Originally, motorbikes were simply bicycles with motors, and personal computers, although smaller and cheaper, were just as difficult to use as larger computers. Similarly, virtual presentations have not been able to shed their reputation for being hastily fashioned materials with just a few more bells and whistles that are poorly utilized by inexperienced facilitators. However, do not let that stop you.

The purpose of this book is to help you develop and deliver rich virtual presentations that audiences will gladly attend and will not forget. Such compelling presentations can increase sales, reduce the time it takes for your employees to get up to speed, and increase the adoption of key corporate initiatives. The types of virtual presentations that you will be able to deliver successfully are *virtually* endless. They include sales presentations, product launches, technical seminars, product demonstrations, company briefings, training courses, impromptu speeches, panels, and roundtables.

This book is for anyone who already conducts or is planning to conduct virtual presentations. In the following pages, you will find tips, ideas, and guidelines for planning and delivering virtual presentations that are interactive and participative, and that achieve business results. This book provides you with quick and pragmatic how-to advice on energizing your virtual presentations. In reading it, you will find (1) convincing evidence that anything you can do in a face-to-face presentation can be duplicated in a virtual presentation, (2) information on the weaknesses of virtual presentations, and how to overcome them, (3) practical strategies for using virtual presentations effectively in everyday situations, and (4) demonstrations of these strategies in real-world situations.

Virtual presentations can be compelling, interactive, and engaging when they are done right. This takes some time and effort (although not *that* much), which is why you are reading this book. We believe that it is not the medium that creates compelling and richly interactive presentations; it is the communication strategies that are utilized. With flexibility and creativity, anything you can do in a physical environment, you can duplicate in a virtual environment. Just try it.

Welcome, and best of luck living and communicating in this virtual world.

NOTE OF CAUTION

This book contains demonstrations using virtual meeting tools (e.g., Adobe Acrobat Connect Pro, WebEx, Microsoft Live Meeting, and GoToMeeting), but it is not designed to teach you how to use a particular tool. Since our goal is to provide you with key guidelines and supporting examples that you can apply to your own unique situation, we have intentionally not provided this information. We also recognize that the market includes a wide variety of platforms, and that any specific information that we could offer would be obsolete by the time this book is printed. You will be able to apply the knowledge and skills that you will gain from this book to any tool. Most manufacturers provide some form of free online training, and you can purchase many fine third-party books and training courses [e.g., *WebEx for Dummies* and *Acrobat Connect Professional Essential Training* (CD) by Tim Plumer].

ACKNOWLEDGMENTS

I am thankful to my acquisitions editor, John Ahern, for recognizing the value of my work; to my development editor, Joseph Berkowitz, for his assistance and patience; and to Pattie Amoroso and Cheryl Hudson for their careful guidance in the editing and production of this work. I offer my gratitude to Caroline Yeager, the first person to publish my writing, and to Dr. Sivasailam Thiagarajan (Thiagi), who introduced me to the Zen of presenting. I would like to thank Dr. Howard Lewis for starting me on exploring this new technology of virtual presentations. Thanks to Courtney Kriebs and Ryan Graham for promoting my initial workshops on the subject. This book would not have been possible without Bonnie Seligson, who tolerated me while I was crafting this manuscript, and our dogs, Hoss and Maddie, who provided me with endless comfort.

I dedicate this book to my mother, Lila Gendelman, who opened my eyes to the beauty of the written word, and to my mentor, Dr. Donald Cook, who taught me everything else.

INTRODUCTION TO VIRTUAL PRESENTATIONS

"Virtual Reality" is a name being slapped on almost anything these days, especially if it's lame.

— Mark Hamilton

Can you imagine conducting a serious business conversation, presenting an important proposal, or interviewing for a new job without being there? Sure you can; in fact, you have probably performed these activities virtually many times in the past. Every day, we communicate in important ways with people whom we cannot see face-to-face. Admit it; you are living a large chunk of your life in a virtual world.

You have already attended many virtual presentations and probably given a few of your own, but how effective were they? Part 1 will start you on a path toward making your virtual presentations as effective as, and more compelling than, face-to-face presentations. It will walk you through the capabilities and limitations of virtual presentations, provide you with guidelines for minimizing the limitations of virtual presentation tools, and clearly explain the powerful tools that are incorporated into commercially available virtual meeting software.

Research on virtual presentations has indicated that they are at least as effective as face-to-face presentations in business-to-business settings (Frost & Sullivan, 2005). I believe that the current research underestimates the increased effectiveness of virtual presentations. Research on new media typically does not study the wide range of capabilities that these media have to offer. It typically measures the difference of two or more media doing the same boring things.

This part of the book contains the following chapters:

Chapter 1: What Are Virtual Presentations?

Chapter 2: Benefits and Capabilities of Virtual Presentations

Chapter 3: Basic Differences between Virtual and Face-to-Face Presentations

Chapter 4: Synchronous and Asynchronous Communication Environments

Chapter 5: When to Consider a Virtual Presentation (and When *Not* To)

Chapter 6: Virtual Presentation Tools

Chapter 7: How Businesses Are Using Virtual Presentations to Increase Their Success

Chapter 8: Challenges in Conducting Virtual Presentations

Chapter 9: Minimizing the Challenges in Conducting Virtual Presentations

Chapter 10: What You Need to Do to Deliver Virtual Presentations That Move People

WHAT ARE VIRTUAL PRESENTATIONS?

Many companies are taking advantage of the new technologies that enable people to communicate using twenty-first-century virtual presentation tools. When you care enough to deliver your message to a large or geographically scattered audience but do not want to travel far and wide to do so, there is no better technique at your disposal.

Business professionals in every industry and organizational function that you can imagine use virtual presentations. They do so in order to establish business relationships, demonstrate products, and stay in touch with analysts and investors. However, there are also many less obvious reasons for going the virtual route, and these include generating leads, enhancing the productivity of research and development, providing cost-effective global training, and even offering customer support. We will go into these uses in more detail in Chapter 7, but let's first discuss what exactly a virtual presentation is. Virtual presentations are presentations that you conduct remotely. The first virtual presentations were teleconferences, but the technology grew from there. In addition to incorporating the speaker's voice, they may now include watching multimedia presentations, chatting with participants, sharing the contents of your screen, and distributing documents, and that is just the beginning.

Virtual presentations can be a powerful instrument. During the initial stage of adopting any new technology, our reaction is typically to use it just as we did the old technology, while happily noticing the slightly faster performance and more colorful features. It usually takes a long time before we figure out that a new medium demands a new approach and that we can use it better and more effectively.

Pilots are taught to fly using two approaches: by sight and by instruments. In the first approach, they can see what is out there and supplement that visual information with the readings of their instruments. When pilots fly by instruments, those readings are all they have. They use those readings to "see" what is out there in the wild blue yonder. These different approaches to flying require different skills. Many of you are already talented face-to-face presenters or you would not be reading this book. Furthermore, you probably became that way from watching other presenters, just like the pilots who learned by sight. In this book, however, you will be learning how to fly using the second approach—when you cannot see anything. But remember, even without "sight," you still have your controls and your instruments, and you're going to become great at using them.

BENEFITS AND CAPABILITIES OF VIRTUAL PRESENTATIONS

Fully utilizing virtual presentations can provide organizations with an enormous return on their investment. There are documented cases in which virtual presentations have reduced decision-making cycles from several months to just 10 days and secured a 235 percent return on investment (ROI) in just two years (Frost & Sullivan, 2005). It's easy to see how such results are achieved when you consider all the benefits that virtual presentations make possible.

BENEFITS

Using virtual presentations has the following benefits:

- **Making maximum use of managers' and executives' time.** In a smoothly running company, everyone should be firing on all cylinders. If key members of management have constant demands for attending meetings and making presentations outside of the office, they may not be able to make the best use of their time. Rather than waste company time and money racking up frequent flyer miles, these managers can conduct presentations from their office and devote more time to putting out logistical fires *without* the aid of a BlackBerry.

- **Accelerating decision making.** Most important decisions are made by groups. In today's fast-paced and geographically dispersed business world, this means fitting travel time into already busy schedules. Using virtual presentations takes travel time out of the equation, making it easier for people to meet sooner and make decisions faster.

- **Enhancing productivity and driving down operating costs.** Having the ability to share information without leaving your desk accelerates every aspect of your operation. It also enhances the productivity of your employees and business partners and drives down your operating costs.

- **Reducing time to market.** Virtual presentations simply enable everything to operate faster. In product development environments, this reduction in time reduces time to market. As we all know, time can often be more valuable than money.

- **Enabling richer and faster communication at Web-based speed.** Virtual presentations exponentially increase business professionals' ability to communicate faster. They also provide people with the ability to share not only voice and text, but also PowerPoint presentations, multimedia, documents, and the contents of their screens. Virtual presentations facilitate this type of communication with employees and business partners across the city, across the country, or around the world.

- **Tapping expertise wherever it resides.** The rich suite of virtual presentation capabilities described later in this chapter allows people to communicate with experts in different geographies with as much richness as if they were in the same room, but without the time and expense associated with national and international travel.

- **Leveling the playing field for small and medium-sized businesses.** Virtual presentations enable small and medium-sized businesses to increase their territory drastically. They now have the ability to provide far-flung customers and business partners with a high-touch experience at a low-touch price. This levels the playing field and gives companies of all shapes and sizes the ability to compete on an equal footing.

- **Troubleshooting IT problems cost-effectively.** Resolving information technology problems effectively typically requires either substantial expense on the part of the provider to travel to the customer location or a great deal of patience on the part of the customer to work with support resources in different states or countries. Virtual presentations can provide both providers of support services and customers with the best of both worlds. Remote resources can extend high-quality support cost-effectively by allowing those providing the support to use virtual presentation tools to see what the customer is seeing while they are working through computer problems.

- **Accommodating the needs of disabled employees.** Some disabilities make it difficult or impossible for employees to drive to work, take the elevator to the appropriate floor and, the Americans with Disabilities Act (ADA) compliance aside, function effectively in a standard business environment. Using virtual presentation technologies, disabled employees can work as productively from home offices as they would from a standard office. Since disabled employees have a variety of ways to communicate (e.g., text or audio), they can use the modality that is easiest for them. I was once director of career services for a university and helped a graduating student start her own multimedia communications company. She progressed quickly and was very successful. Only after we had completed our work did she confide in me that she was a quadriplegic. I had never noticed.

As all these benefits indicate, virtual presentations can be a vital help to any company that has a message to get across. However, if a job is worth doing, then it's worth doing well. With that in mind, it is important to know that when you give a presentation virtually, you can get the job done just as well as if you conducted the presentation in person. To accomplish this, virtual presentations provide you with a rich suite of capabilities that even eclipses those of face-to-face presentation technologies.

CAPABILITIES

The following are possible with virtual presentations:

- **Presenting to hundreds of attendees at the same time.** Virtual presentations can drastically extend your reach to include remote employees, business partners, and even customers located throughout the world.

- **Using one integrated tool.** Most virtual presentation services and applications provide you with one dashboard that you can use to speak to attendees, display PowerPoints, run media presentations, and summarize or collect the group's thoughts on an electronic whiteboard.

- **Storing presentations for future retrieval.** You can easily store virtual presentations. This allows attendees to review the presentation and catch anything that they may have missed. It also enables people who were not able to attend your presentation to view it at their convenience.

- **Presenting in ways that you simply could not use before.**

  - Effectively conduct new types of marketing, promotional, and employee communications events that were not financially feasible using older technologies. This may include sales Webinars to introduce new products to more modest-sized prospects or training sessions for widely dispersed business partners.

  - Support critical business processes such as management decision making and design reviews by enabling attendees to share presentations and review documents in "real time."

  - Enable your organization to meet ad hoc needs, such has conducting emergency status meetings with attendees at distant field offices, within hours instead of days.

  - Enhance your organization's ability to build and maintain closer relationships by enabling richer, more convenient, and less expensive communication.

BASIC DIFFERENCES BETWEEN VIRTUAL AND FACE-TO-FACE PRESENTATIONS

There are many types of presentations in the business world. There are status meetings, sales presentations, briefings, motivational presentations, new product introductions, "dog and pony shows," and the ever-present training sessions. These presentations are meant to inspire, inform, and influence the audience. Fortunately, a great presentation can be given either in person or virtually; however, there are some basic differences between face-to-face and virtual presentations, which is what we will discuss in this chapter.

LOCATION AND TIME

Unlike face-to-face presentations, virtual presentations do not require people to travel to a central facility. Virtual presentations do not need to be scheduled and presented to all participants at the same fixed time. They are much more flexible. Virtual presentations enable participants to attend at the location of their choice, and sometimes at a time of their choosing.

SIZE OF THE AUDIENCE

The size of the audience for a face-to-face presentation is entirely dependent on how much space is available on site. If you have the use of only the small conference room down the hall, then you can play to only five to ten people at a time. With virtual presentations, on the other hand, the sky is the limit. While face-to-face presentations can accommodate a limited number of participants, a virtual presentation can accommodate audiences of all shapes and sizes. Sure, bandwidth may constrain the number of attendees at a virtual presentation, but in most cases, you can address these constraints simply by adding more lines.

CONTENT DELIVERY TOOLS

Physical presentations typically involve the presenters themselves, computers, a liquid crystal display (LCD) projector, VCRs or DVDs, flipcharts, and whiteboards. Virtual presentations incorporate electronic versions of these tools, along with a few more. They include breakout rooms (virtual areas where you can place attendees when you want to separate them into groups), e-mail, chats, electronic whiteboards (screens where attendees can write down their thoughts—sort of like an electronic flipchart that everyone can use), discussion boards, shared folders, and online Web-based resources such as Web sites and blogs. Some of these terms may be unfamiliar to you, but we will go into each of them in more detail when we explore the virtual presentation tools.

MODES OF COMMUNICATION

Physical presentations support a variety of communication modes, including face-to-face spoken communication, visual aids, text, PowerPoint, and other types of multimedia presentations. While virtual presentations rely more upon textual tools, such as chats, e-mails, and whiteboard entries, do not consider this a strict limitation. All Shakespeare had was words, and he did a good job with them! Great comedians and storytellers transport you into a completely new world by weaving a complex tapestry of words. So, do not feel limited. And remember, you do have many tools other than text, and in this book, we will teach you how to use them.

SYNCHRONOUS AND ASYNCHRONOUS COMMUNICATION ENVIRONMENTS

When it comes time to plan your virtual presentation, you can choose to conduct it in one of two ways: synchronously or asynchronously. A phone call is an example of a *synchronous* communication. Both parties can hear and respond to each other right then and there. E-mail is an example of *asynchronous*, or one-way, communication. You can ask a colleague a question at 8 a.m. and review her response at 8 p.m. that night.

When your virtual presentation is synchronous, it allows your audience to listen and respond in real time. In such virtual presentations, all participants are attending at the same time, as though they were in the same room together. In an asynchronous virtual presentation, you may post a discussion topic in the morning, and participants may send their responses throughout the day. The ability to unite a scattered audience at the same time is one of the key benefits of giving a virtual presentation. Both methods have their respective benefits, which we address here.

BENEFITS OF ASYNCHRONOUS COMMUNICATION

- **It accommodates different schedules.** Asynchronous virtual presentations can support people who have atypical schedules. Workers may be able to spare an hour only in the morning, before the office gets crazy-busy, or free up some time only in the evening once their children are asleep. In these situations, asynchronous communications can work very well. As mentioned earlier, e-mail and posting discussion topics are examples of asynchronous communication.

- **It allows more in-depth responses.** An asynchronous communication provides readers with more time for reflection. Since people are not communicating with one another in real time, everyone will have more time to think about the presentation and prepare more thorough, well-considered answers to their questions.

- **Asynchronous presentations are used predominantly in education.** Currently, distance leaning is the largest user of asynchronous communications. It provides people who have full-time jobs or are homemakers with the ability to complete their studies at times that are convenient for them. It would be extremely difficult for such nontraditional students to complete their education using a face-to-face approach.

WHEN TO CONSIDER A VIRTUAL PRESENTATION (AND WHEN NOT TO)

As the author of a book about conducting virtual presentations, I have an obvious bias toward presenting virtually whenever possible. Having said that, though, I am a pragmatist: there are going to be times when giving a virtual presentation would not be the best way to go. In most cases, I would encourage you to consider conducting a virtual presentation, but there are definitely circumstances that call for the tried-and-true technique of presenting face-to-face. Here is a breakdown of times when you should consider a virtual presentation and times when you should not.

WHEN VIRTUAL PRESENTATIONS ARE A MUST

Virtual presentations should be conducted when you:

- **Need to present to more than 25 people at the same time.** As stated previously, there is only so much space in a conference room. Whenever you need to send a message to the entire floor or the entire company, your best bet is to go virtual.

- **Need to reach people far away (cheaply).** If it's in your company's best interest to keep the travel budget low, then a virtual presentation can get your message across while saving a fortune in airfare. Virtual presentations will enable you to reach larger and more dispersed audiences that you may not have been able to reasonably accommodate in the past.

- **Have serious stage fright.** Some people are excellent communicators in certain settings, but are deathly afraid of being in the spotlight. They are great on the phone, but not so good face-to-face. Although programs like Toastmasters can be beneficial in the long term for helping such people improve at presenting in person, in the short term, a virtual presentation is ideal.

- **Need the more advanced capabilities of virtual presentations.** You should consider using virtual if it would be beneficial to archive your presentation for viewing by those who were not able to attend in person. A virtual presentation may also benefit your organization by establishing and maintaining a cohesive group of participants (e.g., a community of practice) who stay in touch after your presentation. Finally, using frequent virtual presentations may foster collaboration and build stronger teams.

WHEN FACE-TO-FACE PRESENTATIONS ARE A MUST

Face-to-face presentations should be conducted when you:

- **Have bad news to deliver.** If the meeting is about something that is deeply emotional, such as an announcement that layoffs are forthcoming or that performance has been poor all-around this quarter (and hopefully that isn't the case for anyone reading this book!), then the message needs to be delivered in person. Many people feel that finding out bad news on a computer screen feels like a slap in the face on top of the bad news itself. It's better to conduct these kinds of meetings face-to-face.

- **Need to establish trust.** A crucial objective of many meetings is to establish trust. Presentations designed to engender investor confidence or an unquenchable desire for a new product would be a couple of examples. Establishing trust requires engaging many of the attendees' senses. Visual cues and social presence are critical to building trust. These two elements are usually missing from a virtual presentation. They can be achieved only by someone who is highly skilled in the art and science of virtual presenting. After reading this book, though, you may become a member of this elite group.

- **Need to change attitudes.** Conducting a presentation that can change people's attitudes is difficult to pull off in person and nearly impossible in a virtual environment. As with building trust, visual cues and social presence are critical here. To succeed, these presentations not only need to establish trust, but must create an environment that is intimate, open, and accepting. After all, you might have to call people out on the carpet regarding their current attitudes before you explain the need for change. You may attempt such a feat virtually with an audience of people who are already familiar with one another and are committed to the tasks at hand, but even then, you need to tread carefully.

TAKE ACTION

Now that you have had an opportunity to read this chapter, taking into consideration your company and its partners and customers, when would you consider using virtual presentations and when would you not? Take a moment now to review and consider your own presentations. Use Table 5.1 to identify those presentations that you would consider converting to virtual presentations and those that you would not.

TABLE 5.1 TAKE ACTION FORM: USES OF VIRTUAL MEETINGS

Presentations That I Would Consider Converting to Virtual	Presentations That I Would Not Consider Converting to Virtual

VIRTUAL PRESENTATION TOOLS

Virtual presentations are supported by various services and applications that are available on the market. Currently, the major players are Adobe Acrobat Connect Pro, WebEx, Microsoft Live Meeting, and GoToMeeting. Anything that I could say about these particular tools may be outdated by the time you read this book, but at least you'll have an idea of what sort of tools to look for in your virtual presentation software. There are no slouches in the bunch. I could go into further detail, but this book is not meant to compare the various virtual presentation services and applications or to train you on how to use them. There are a wealth of articles, white papers, books, and Internet resources that can help you with your product research.

Whichever one you decide on, though, most services incorporate several of the same powerful tools that you can use to create and deliver your virtual presentations. In this chapter, you will find a broad overview of what these tools are and how you might use them. At the end of the chapter, you'll find a sample screen from a virtual presentation that shows what these tools look like in action.

TOOLS FOR DISPLAYING OR CONTROLLING MEDIA

Picture Window

You can share a video stream of yourself while you present or insert a picture of yourself. Another option is to mix things up by showing a photograph of selected participants as they interact with the group, demonstrate an application, or answer a question.

Audio Control

Participants may use this control to turn their audio on and off or adjust the level. I typically recommend that both you and your attendees use either a computer or telephone headset to increase the quality of the audio and avoid disrupting others.

Presentation Window

This tool enables you to share a PowerPoint or media presentation with the group. Other media may include a high-end promotional piece, a video demonstration, or a YouTube.

Screen Sharing

You may share your desktop or a portion of your screen with attendees. Sharing your desktop means that attendees will be able to see what you are seeing on your screen or on a portion of your screen. With your permission, participants may also share their screens with you and with other colleagues who are attending your virtual presentation. They may view notations that you place on your screen, such as arrows and other methods of highlighting. You may also share a variety of media, including photographs, slide shows, and animations.

TOOLS FOR INTERACTING WITH PARTICIPANTS

Chat

During your virtual presentation, you can exchange instant messages and e-mails with participants with the chat function. You can also send group messages and e-mails during a presentation. In addition, you may use chats to engage in written dialogue with participants or promote discussion among attendees. I recommend avoiding chats among participants, except during discussions and some exercise activities, as they can often go off topic. Most virtual presentation services and applications allow you to control who may chat with whom. You can also control which chats may be displayed to the rest of the group. You, your producer/moderator, and other presenters may also communicate privately, without the attendees viewing your chats.

Participants' Window

The participants' window is more than just a roll call for attendees. It is typically located to the side of the whiteboard. This window displays the names of the people attending the presentation and several icons that they may use to provide you with feedback. The icons typically include

✔ for Yes, ✘ for No, a raised hand for "I have a question," and clapping hands to let you know that you are doing a good job.

Polling

During the presentation, you may ask a question and allow participants to vote on a single choice (e.g., "How many of you feel that this presentation is relevant to your current situation?"). This is a good way to check participants' interest and engagement in your virtual presentation. Taking polls involves the members of your audience and keeps them interested. It's also a good way to get feedback on how you're doing as a presenter, and you might learn something from it. You can display or not display the results of the poll to the rest of the attendees.

Whiteboard

The whiteboard serves the same function as a flipchart in a face-to-face meeting—it provides you with a blank screen that either you or the attendees can type or draw on. This is a bit different from screen sharing. Instead of enabling attendees to share the contents of their screen, this tool enables participants to simply add their comments to a blank screen. Use the whiteboard as the electronic equivalent of a flipchart, not an LCD projector.

Shared Folders

Shared folders are electronic locations where you can store documents, media, and even other presentations for participants to download and refer to. These materials may include PowerPoint slides, assignments, notes, lists of resources and Web sites, answers to frequently asked questions (FAQs), and other documents. You may request that participants review this information prior to, during, or after your presentation.

Figure 6.1 shows a sample screen from a virtual meeting that illustrates most of these tools.

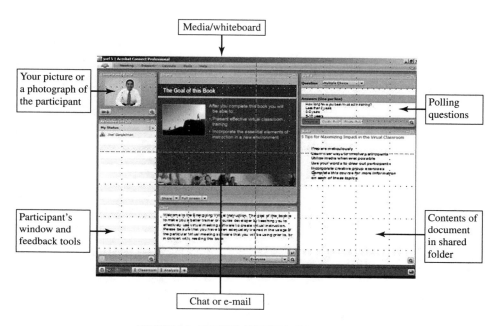

FIGURE 6.1: VIRTUAL PRESENTATION SCREEN

As stated before, virtual meeting applications have several screen templates that you can use. You also have the ability to fine-tune the screen layout, such as moving or adding windows. Now that you know what tools and applications are part of a virtual presentation, let's take a look at the myriad ways your organization can use virtual presentations.

HOW BUSINESSES ARE USING VIRTUAL PRESENTATIONS TO INCREASE THEIR SUCCESS

Virtual presentations have become a standard communication tool in just about every industry and department. People use them in many different ways to enhance the efficiency with which they conduct business. In this chapter, we will explore how companies are benefiting from using virtual presentations as a strategic business tool. You may wish to choose some of the usages that we have identified for the presentations that your own department conducts. The following examples may give you some ideas of how you can use virtual presentations to solidify your organization's future success.

HOW MAJOR INDUSTRIES ARE USING VIRTUAL PRESENTATIONS

Financial Services

Financial services companies use virtual presentations to accelerate the speed of product rollouts. They use virtual presentations to quickly provide information on the specifics of new products to salespeople and business partners, such as brokers. These organizations also utilize the capabilities of virtual presentations to accelerate loan processing, ensure compliance, communicate with prospective clients, and provide personalized customer service.

Health Care

These days everyone is talking about increasing the effectiveness of health care. Well, virtual presentations can help. Using virtual presentations, remote specialists can collaborate with local practitioners to diagnose rare diseases. Medical professionals can also utilize virtual presentations to reduce the efforts and expense required to maintain regulatory requirements (e.g., the Health Insurance Portability and Accountability Act, or HIPPA) and more easily engage high-level management at health-care facilities in decision making.

High Technology

High-technology companies are a natural for using virtual presentations. Many use such presentations to enhance discussions with customers, business partners, and vendors. These meetings can substantially accelerate time-critical deadlines and product launches. High-technology companies also make extensive use of virtual meetings to reach out to prospects by sharing industry knowledge and business information. They also employ virtual presentation capabilities to provide rapid and cost-effective technical support.

Manufacturing Firms

Manufacturing firms certainly use virtual presentations to collaborate with suppliers, technicians, dealers, employees, and customers. They also use virtual presentations to enhance cooperation among engineers, train salespeople, and keep prospects engaged throughout the sales cycle.

Educational Institutions

Finally, educational institutions use virtual presentations extensively to provide distance education and keep high-level professionals with demanding schedules (e.g., doctors) current on new research and practices.

HOW KEY DEPARTMENTS ARE USING VIRTUAL PRESENTATIONS

Many companies and departments are scaling back on travel costs as a way to reduce operating expenses. Some people are overjoyed by this news, because it means that they can spend less time away from home and more time with their family. As I've said before, virtual presentations can reduce costs and keep employees happier and closer to home. However, if they aren't handled correctly, virtual presentations can turn into teleconferences, where no one says anything and everyone just kind of sits there and listens. Such experiences really don't help you, your department, or your organization. In order to provide value, virtual meetings need to work—that is, they need to accomplish business objectives, foster communication, and build stronger relationships. Within all industries, virtual presentations support not only the general needs of the company as a whole, but also the more specific needs of key departments, including sales, marketing, customer support, training, product development, corporate communications, and human resources.

Table 7.1 summarizes how a wide variety of departments are using virtual presentations to operate not only faster and more cheaply, but in ways that enable them to achieve the goals of their organization more effectively. Take a moment to review how virtual presentations can help your organization not simply by allowing it to do more with less, but by doing things differently. You may get a few ideas of your own.

TABLE 7.1 HOW DEPARTMENTS ARE USING VIRTUAL PRESENTATIONS

Department	How It Is Using Virtual Presentations
All departments	More rapid decision making.
	Enhance global operations by conducting more convenient and more frequent presentations with geographically dispersed personnel.
	Enhance collaboration among departments and team members.
	Deploy critical knowledge rapidly.
	Bridge geographical and company boundaries, while seamlessly including suppliers, consultants, and other third-party stakeholders.
	Provide increased access to experts and other resources throughout the world.
Sales	Provide prospects with a high-touch selling experience at a low-touch cost. (In some cases, this Web-touch selling has increased sales by 250 percent and reduced the sales cycle from one year to six months.)
	Present to prospects that it would not be economically feasible to call on using traditional means.
	Generate leads through online events, such as free educational Webinars and virtual conferences.
	Support more territory and more customers, and generate greater sales.
	Increase the number of calls per salesperson.
	Drastically reduce the cost of a sales call. In one documented case, this cost was reduced from $3,700

(*Continued*)

TABLE 7.1 (CONTINUED)

Department	How It Is Using Virtual Presentations
	to $750 by eliminating the cost and time required to travel to customer locations.
	Increase the close rate by reacting faster than the competition.
	Reduce scheduling delays and travel time.
	Respond to inquiries more quickly.
	Instantly deliver compelling presentations around the globe.
	Conveniently conduct richer sales meetings, kick-offs, training sessions, and product launches.
	Provide more time and tools to build closer and stronger customer relationships.
	Get the "right" people (decision makers, product specialists, company executives, technical gurus) involved in a sale sooner.
	Resolve sales issues more quickly, since more people can get together sooner and more conveniently.
	Get your message out to prospects and existing customers faster.
	Accelerate the review of contracts.
Marketing	Generate a larger number of qualified leads with targeted, compelling Webinars and events.
	Increase your contact with customers, analysts, and prospects by conducting frequent virtual interactions.
	Conduct virtual marketing, promotional, and awareness events, including Webinars with industry experts on timely topics.
	Conduct more effective remote reviews with geographically distributed agencies, contractors, and marketing teams.

(Continued)

TABLE 7.1 (CONTINUED)

Department	How It Is Using Virtual Presentations
	Easily create an on-demand repository of virtual presentations. Effectively support online product launch events that can reach a broad audience with a consistent message.
Customer support	Provide faster and more efficient responses to customers. Reduce support costs, including travel time and expense. Enable technical support personnel to easily access remote computers anywhere in the world. Aid support personnel in quickly diagnosing problems, transferring files, and installing patches and updates. Reduce call handling time by giving technicians the ability to see the customer's screen. Eliminate the frustrating back-and-forth handling of support issues by immediately involving quality assurance and research and development personnel.
Training	Support product rollouts more effectively by improving the readiness of salespeople and partners through deploying training faster, more conveniently, more cost-effectively, and to a wider audience. Decrease the cost and time overhead for traveling to training. Provide more targeted, granular, and ad hoc training. Deliver richer, engaging, effective, and cost-efficient training courses to internal personnel, channel partners, and customers. Increase the availability of training to a widening global audience. Increase the availability and profitability of customer training.

(Continued)

TABLE 7.1 (CONTINUED)

Department	How It Is Using Virtual Presentations
Product development	Shorten product design cycles by eliminating scheduling delays, reducing travel time, and providing access to key resources. Support seamless collaboration with partners, customers, and distributors. Accelerate projects and time to market by enabling design teams to meet frequently and interact with rich media and 3D data to review and interactively revise designs.
Human resources	Communicate benefit changes, options, and government regulations easily and explain new programs to employees.
Company meetings	Enable corporate executives to communicate with employees easily and more frequently.
Information technology	Instantly escalate employee support calls to an online support session. Support distributed users from any location by remotely controlling their desktops to see and fix problems in real time. Shorten the time required for application rollouts by supporting teams in setting requirements, prototype testing, joint development, and system launch. Track progress among multiple teams by enabling more frequent, more substantive, and more collaborative project status meetings. Accelerate the deployment of new business-critical software by reducing the time required to train users from several months to a few weeks.
Senior management	Enable a geographically dispersed management team to review proposals, collaborate on important content, and keep projects moving forward.

(Continued)

TABLE 7.1 (CONTINUED)

Department	How It Is Using Virtual Presentations
Research and development and manufacturing	Provide customers with virtual access to high-level engineering resources, regardless of their location. Meet and communicate frequently with partner and supplier networks to update business trends, provide education and road maps, and keep the entire supply chain in sync.

TAKE ACTION

Now that you have had an opportunity to review how a wide range of industries and departments are using virtual presentations to enhance their success, how will you be using them?

Take a moment now to thumb through Table 7.1 and make some notes for yourself in Table 7.2, identifying the types of virtual presentations that you would like to conduct immediately and in the near term (within three to six months).

TABLE 7.2 TAKE ACTION FORM: USES OF VIRTUAL MEETINGS

Immediate Uses	Near-Term Uses

CHALLENGES IN CONDUCTING VIRTUAL PRESENTATIONS

In the previous chapter, we discussed what businesses in some very different industries stand to gain from using virtual presentations. Over the next two chapters, we will be taking a look at what may be preventing certain companies from getting on board and how they might get around those issues. You may have the impression that virtual presentations come with a long list of limitations. Quite the contrary! While there are some elements of a face-to-face presentation that simply cannot be duplicated, you will find that virtual presentations offer a lot of powerful substitutes. Nevertheless, let us get those perceived limitations out of the way.

Virtual presentations have some significant limitations, including lack of visual clues, diminished ability to build rapport and trust, technological challenges, outside distractions, reduced attention spans, minimized ability for participants to control the presentation, greater challenge to maintain participant focus, more difficulty in controlling and directing participants, reduced access to presenters, greater difficulty in encouraging participation, and challenges in accommodating different communication styles.

LACK OF VISUAL CUES

Given that more than 85 percent of human communication is nonverbal, it is typically important that you see the person you're speaking with in business. A lot of people seem to have the misconception that the visual cues associated with face-to-face communication cannot be duplicated in virtual presentations. After all, out of our five senses, we rely most on our visual sense and feel lost when it is unavailable. It is true that in a virtual presentation you may not always see what the presenter is doing, as he will be visually tucked away into a corner of your screen. However, a smart presenter will use a variety of techniques to make sure that he has the attention of the audience.

DIMINISHED ABILITY TO BUILD RAPPORT AND TRUST

Social presence is the degree to which a communications medium allows participants to feel connected to others and establish trust. In face-to-face presentations, we have a great deal of social presence, which allows us to build trust. Skilled face-to-face presenters do this through their proximity to members of the audience, their facial expressions, and their body language. The absence of visual and physical contact during virtual presentations reduces social presence and makes it more difficult to build rapport and trust between presenters and participants, as well as among the participants themselves.

This lack of social presence makes it easier for someone who doesn't want to follow along to detach. While some people instinctively want to be recognized, others prefer to remain anonymous. Virtual presentations allow these people to sit on the sidelines and stay silent. Skilled virtual presenters are well aware of this tendency and use the extensive capabilities of virtual presentations to draw out these participants. However, it's important to note that there are people in every meeting who would prefer to remain invisible and resent being dragged out of their comfortable cocoon—and a virtual presentation gives them the opportunity to do so. Try to avoid providing them with that opportunity.

TECHNOLOGICAL CHALLENGES

One of the main fears that people have regarding virtual presentations is that a technical malfunction could occur during a meeting and derail the whole show. Technology can be very temperamental, as we all know. It's not always available, and sometimes it does not work the way it's expected to—and that can and does happen when the stakes are high. There may be issues with software applications at the desktop level and/or network connectivity problems or delays. The competence of both the presenter and the participants with the hardware and software can vary considerably, leading to many variations of foul-ups. Even something as simple as the speed at which someone can type during a text-based chat session may alter the effectiveness of your virtual presentation. Finally, the more complex the technology, the more opportunities there are for a malfunction. Simply put, there's a lot that can go wrong.

Of course, there's also a lot that can go wrong during an in-person presentation as well. Anyone who's ever had to deal with a finicky laptop or a broken LCD projector can attest to this. There are always chances for things to go wrong during *any* kind of presentation. Your best defense against this limitation is to overprepare and always have a backup plan when the stakes are high.

DISTRACTIONS

External Distractions

Office life will continue as usual around the person who is viewing a virtual presentation, and this can be a major problem. The environment surrounding attendees will probably be distracting, depending on the time of day or the day of the week. Coworkers will continue talking; telephones will continue ringing.

Internal Distractions

In the twenty-first century, we have become a very distractible society. Sometimes it seems that everyone nowadays has attention deficit disorder. Plop us in front of a TV, and we'll blaze through every channel available. Give us Wi-Fi, and we'll jump from Web site to Web site. Which brings us to the problem of participating in a presentation at our desk. The idea of checking e-mail and performing other work tasks can be very tempting. Multitasking during a virtual presentation is all too common, and it can interfere with someone's reception of the message that the presenter is trying to get across. Also, there is a greater chance of getting an eyes-glazed-over feeling when concentrating through a computer monitor, as opposed to a conference room setting with a lot of people around. This fatigue places a strain on participants' already short attention spans.

GREATER CHALLENGE TO MAINTAIN PARTICIPANT FOCUS

Typically, we as presenters use the visual realm to keep attendees interested in us. We dress well, look them in the eye, make gestures with our hands, and use a variety of facial expressions. On the flip side, we also use our visual sense to monitor whether people are disengaged, based on their nonverbal feedback, and then we adjust our presentation as needed to recapture their attention. Maintaining and monitoring the focus of the attendees in virtual presentations is difficult, but possible.

You can keep a remote audience interested and involved; just make sure you don't go overboard. In trying to provide an engaging experience using a variety of approaches (e.g., video clips, multiple chat strings, and polling), it is possible to overwhelm participants. This is especially true in presentations attended by a large number of attendees.

MORE DIFFICULTY IN DIRECTING AND CONTROLLING PARTICIPANTS

Nonverbal techniques, such as eye contact and physical proximity, are effective in managing participants in face-to-face presentations. It is also possible to physically arrange a traditional presentation environment based upon the nature of the activities, such as using round tables for group discussions. Since you probably will not have eye contact and it is more difficult to improvise in a virtual presentation, managing and directing participants is more challenging.

REDUCED ACCESS TO PARTICIPANTS

In general, presenters may not feel as available to participants in virtual presentations as they are in more traditional face-to-face presentations. For instance, even if a hand does not go up during an in-person presentation, the presenter can usually pick up whether the audience understands the message. That feeling does not translate exactly to virtual presentations. Therefore, attendees may need to feel that they have more ongoing support from you, or they may feel more isolated. This problem can be addressed by checking in with the audience frequently to see whether there are any questions or difficulties.

GREATER DIFFICULTY IN ENCOURAGING PARTICIPATION

The audience can see the presenter, but the presenter cannot see the audience. A virtual presentation is one-sided in that respect. Attendees must therefore be more autonomous and self-directed. Effective virtual presenters need to provide sufficient variety, encouragement, and interaction to ensure that attendees are fully engaged.

DIFFICULTY IN ACCOMMODATING DIFFERENT COMMUNICATION STYLES

In some ways it is easier and in some ways more difficult for virtual presentations to accommodate people with different communication styles, since they do not allow for quite as many methods of communication as face-to-face presentations. For instance, someone who is very expressive with her body language and gestures will have to find a new way to get her points across.

TAKE ACTION

While there are a ton of benefits from conducting virtual presentations, there are certainly some challenges. What would be the greatest challenges to you, and why?

Use Table 8.1 to record the three largest challenges that you face and what makes them so significant.

TABLE 8.1 TAKE ACTION FORM: CHALLENGES IN CONDUCTING VIRTUAL PRESENTATIONS

Challenges		Why This Is a Significant Challenge
Challenge 1		
Challenge 2		
Challenge 3		

MINIMIZING THE CHALLENGES IN CONDUCTING VIRTUAL PRESENTATIONS

Now, how can you minimize some of the challenges in virtual presentations? Here are a few countermeasures that you can use to get beyond any of the hurdles that you might find in your way. Rather than addressing each individual limitation on its own terms, what follows is a general guide to overcoming these perceived limitations. Any of the efforts identified here can reduce the effects of one or more of the challenges presented in the previous chapter.

USE WHAT YOU'VE GOT

Create a captivating, fun, and meaningful presentation environment by taking full advantage of the capabilities of virtual presentations. You may engage participants' minds by drawing out and incorporating exciting "real-world" examples and contemporary content. Become a master at using your virtual presentation service or application. Don't just conduct a telephone conference. Learn how to use capabilities such as the electronic whiteboard, polling, and chat. Modern virtual presentation services and applications offer you a wealth of tools. Learn them and use them to enhance the success of your virtual presentations.

SET THE TONE ON YOUR TERMS

Both at the beginning and throughout a presentation, it's important that you set the tone in terms of level of formality and maintaining respect. There are many ways to accomplish this feat that are covered in this book, and here are just a few of them. When conducting your presentation, you probably want to maintain the same casualness and tone of voice that you are using now. Always insist on attendees respecting you and other participants. At its most basic level, respect involves not making negative statements about others or denigrating their contributions. It also includes allowing others to speak and valuing their comments. In short, insist upon good manners. Do not allow side conversations that can easily turn into chatter and gossip. Setting the tone of your presentation up front will reduce problems later on and ensure that your virtual presentations run smoothly.

KEEP IT SHORT AND SWEET

Reduce the length of your presentation as much as possible. Keep it to a minimal length so that you can maximize the audience members' attention while they are all sitting by their computers with Internet access one tantalizing click away. When it comes to a time limit, 60 to 90 minutes is tops for a virtual presentation. Some presentations can go as long as two hours, but only if it is essential to go on that long—and if it is, the presentation had better be very visual, include multiple presenters and a great deal of interaction, and be flawlessly delivered. These days people have the attention span of a flea, so keep your presentations brief and to the point. You will find that they work better.

MAKE IT ALL ABOUT THE AUDIENCE

Focus your presentation on the needs of your audience rather than your own needs. Cover the "right stuff"—the topics that attendees are interested in and that are close to their hearts. Addressing these kinds of concerns will make it more likely that you will foster a personal connection. For instance, if you're leading a meeting about a new computer system that is being implemented to replace the notoriously disliked old one, do not go on about how much money the replacement is saving the company in write-offs—focus instead on the problems with the old system that will now be eliminated. You will go further in accomplishing your goals by focusing on the needs of your audience. Give your listeners what they came for. Provide attendees with the skills and information that they are seeking in the way that is most digestible to them. Focus in on their problems and the benefits that they are yearning for.

USE MORE VISUALS AND LESS TEXT

Do not use your PowerPoints as an outline of what you want to say; use them as a series of visuals to support your main points. Again, your presentation should transcend your outline and the things you intend to say. Your presentation is not just about getting your points across for the sake of compliance; it is for your attendees, and it is supposed to ensure that your ideas are 100 percent clear to them. What will help to ensure clarity is using graphics that enable the audience to envision concepts and see relationships. Use visuals instead of text whenever possible.

There are three types of visuals that you can use in a presentation: representational, mnemonic, and explanatory. Representational visuals show what objects look like. Mnemonic visuals help attendees remember certain concepts. And explanatory visuals are, well, self-explanatory. This last category of visuals is probably the most important of the group, since these visuals really convey the points that the presenter is making. Explanatory visuals are further separated into organizational, relational, and transformational visuals. Here is a bit about each.

- **Organizational visuals.** Organizational visuals illustrate relationships. These images are very useful, and they are great for introductions and summaries. The use of icons to illustrate a topic or a concept is an example of an organizational visual. These visuals are a wonderful way to dress up a display. They can be signposts that tell participants where they are in the sequence of your presentation.

- **Relational visuals.** Relational visuals describe numeric and quantitative information. These visuals include pie charts and bar graphs. When you need to get across raw, hard data, but you want a visual component to help make the numbers concrete, a relational visual is the absolute best way to go.

- **Transformational visuals.** Transformational visuals illustrate how things change over time. One example of a transformational visual is a timeline, such as one showing the relationship between artistic styles and historical events. These visuals are successful in the same way that before and after photos are successful in selling weight-loss products to prospective dieters—they really drive home the point that the presenter is making.

When you use visuals, be sure to keep them simple. Fight your initial impulse to make them too comprehensive. Simplify them to highlight your most salient points. You will find that small bits of information are easier for attendees to comprehend. Using relevant and easy-to-digest visuals properly will dramatically increase the effectiveness of your virtual presentations.

GET PEOPLE ACTIVELY ENGAGED

Most attendees do not plan to bring a pillow to your presentation, but later feel sorry that they did not. An effective virtual presentation involves more than just presenting. The single most important element to remember in creating and delivering virtual presentations that work is interactivity. Presenters should conduct frequent and meaningful interactions. You do not have to worry about this now. Chapter 23, "Promoting Interaction," is devoted to just that, and you will also receive hints and ideas on how to build interaction into your virtual presentation throughout this book.

ENCOURAGE PARTICIPATION

You will probably not receive as much feedback during a virtual presentation as you would in a face-to-face presentation, but you will get some. Encourage attendees to participate by sending them chat messages. Be sure to compliment them on their participation. Periodically ask members of the audience if they can see the visuals clearly and if you are moving too fast or too slowly. Remember that the audience members are your eyes and ears. If you want to get over the cold distance of the computer screen that separates you from the members of your audience, you must continually engage them and make sure that they're paying attention.

MAINTAIN A BRISK PACE

A man's reach should exceed his grasp

—Robert Browning

This advice is tough to carry out, but it can make a huge difference in the attendees' enjoyment. Members of your audience will arrive with different abilities and levels of knowledge related to your topic, and some people are simply quicker than others. On top of that, absolutely nobody likes to listen to someone droning on, so it's important that you speak at a quickened, yet unhurried-sounding pace. Try to gauge the speed that is comfortable for the average member of your audience and then pick it up just a notch. Maintaining a brisk pace during your virtual presentation will keep your participants awake, but not frustrated or lost.

DO NOT BE DULL!

This is another piece of advice that's easier said than done, that's for sure. But you can handle it. You are an interesting person with a compelling message. As an accomplished professional, you have a lot to offer the audience, and you don't want people to tune out because you sound too formal or detached. It's best to speak in a conversational tone, but since you are excited about what you do, you should reflect that excitement in your tone and phrasing. Use metaphors and similes. Create word pictures. Tell stories. Above all, do not simply read your presentation. Attendees are always looking for events that are not just useful, but interesting and exciting. With the help of this book, you can ensure that these well-attended events are your own.

If there is only one thing that I hope you embrace from reading this book, it is that virtual presentations can be as dynamic, interactive, and compelling as face-to-face presentations and then some. You simply have to think a bit more and be more creative. You are limited only by your own imagination.

TAKE ACTION

Consider a virtual presentation that you are presenting or plan to present in the near future. Think about what you will do to minimize the major

TABLE 9.1 TAKE ACTION FORM: MINIMIZING THE CHALLENGES OF CONDUCTING VIRTUAL PRESENTATIONS

	How Will You Accomplish This?
Reduce its length	_____ _____ _____
Keenly focus on the needs of attendees	_____ _____ _____
Use more visuals	_____ _____ _____
Get attendees actively engaged	_____ _____ _____

challenges of virtual presentations listed in the left-hand column of Table 9.1 by specifically identifying in the right-hand column how you will handle those challenges. Be as specific as you can by referring to the guidelines identified in this chapter.

WHAT YOU NEED TO DO TO DELIVER VIRTUAL PRESENTATIONS THAT MOVE PEOPLE

At this point in your reading, you probably have a pretty good idea of what virtual presentations are and the benefits that you and your company can derive from them. You are reading this book because you want to learn how to master this new medium. What you'll find in this chapter are a few ideas and strategies that can greatly tip the scales in your favor. Not all of these may seem natural at first, but in time they will feel like second nature. These tips will help make your virtual presentations compelling and drive people to action.

SELECT A GREAT PRODUCER/MODERATOR

In some cases, the presenter of a virtual presentation is responsible for everything. Except for the most ad hoc and casual presentations, I believe that this approach is often a mistake. I recommend that for most important virtual presentations, you consider using a producer/moderator to help you with some of the technical aspects of your virtual presentations and help you liven them up. A solid producer/moderator can be truly helpful in making your virtual presentation a major success. The list of qualifications is a bit of a tall order, but all of these skills can be learned. The producer/moderator should be able to handle the technical aspects of your session and all of the tools involved. His responsibilities include loading and troubleshooting your presentation and supporting materials, setting up breakout rooms, guiding participants in how to use the virtual meeting tools, and recording the session.

In addition to his technical duties, the producer/moderator also functions as an announcer, introducing you and the other presenters, holding questions until a convenient time, restating those questions, monitoring the timing of breaks, and ensuring that everyone has a chance to communicate. Another duty of the producer/moderator is to clarify and enforce the ground rules of the presentation, such as respect in chats. A comprehensive list of ground rules is discussed Chapter 18.

A great producer/moderator is also a valued sidekick. Every great late night host had a gifted sideman. Johnny Carson had Ed McMahon, Gracie Allen had George Burns, and Jay Leno has Kevin Eubanks. What made them uniquely wonderful was their interplay with the host, and that is what you should aim to recreate with your moderator in your own virtual presentations. Begin discussions by directing questions to the moderator, and use his answer as a gateway to some light banter. A little comfortable and casual conversation will go a long way toward bringing some levity to the proceedings. Be sure to select a producer/moderator who complements your style, and keep rehearsing until you zig and zag together.

For smaller and more casual virtual presentations, you may not have the opportunity to have a producer/narrator, and you will need to play that role yourself. This may diminish some of the richness that a good producer/narrator brings to the party, and it increases your responsibility for being comfortable with the technology.

CONSIDER A SEPARATE PRODUCER AND MODERATOR FOR LARGE AUDIENCES

Sometimes, especially if your virtual presentation is attended by a large number of people (several hundred), you may select a producer to handle the technical aspects of this role, and another person to be the moderator. In these instances, the moderator would be more of an MC or announcer, as we have described earlier in this chapter.

REHEARSE, REHEARSE, AND REHEARSE SOME MORE

Effective presentations do not happen by accident—they are the product of rigorous preparation. Your mantra in the lead-up to the big day should be rehearse, rehearse, and then rehearse some more. The more you rehearse, the more spontaneous you can be the day of your virtual presentation. After all, once you have the basics down, you'll know where you can color outside of the lines and be spontaneous.

There is no substitute for rehearsal time. If every technical element goes as smoothly as possible but the presenter sounds unfocused and rambling, that is how the presentation will be remembered. Rehearsing is the only way to work out timing, find the right words, and become comfortable with the transitions and segues between talking points. An audience can easily distinguish between a presenter who is confident, unrushed, and unflustered and one who is struggling with phrasing and pacing.

Rehearsals should include both solo and group preparation. In solo rehearsals, each speaker practices alone and uses the technology to deliver her full presentation aloud as if there were an audience listening. Solo rehearsals should include timings, transitions, and demonstrations. In additional to solo rehearsals, I recommend at least one group rehearsal, including your producer/moderator and all the presenters. I also urge you to consider an additional dry run a couple of days before your presentation that includes a few colleagues to act as attendees.

BE METICULOUS ABOUT THE TECHNICAL DETAILS

Verify the technical details of your presentation environment and your attendees far in advance of the presentation. Test everything, including your PowerPoints, media assets, URLs, and stored handouts, several times. Test the instructions that you provide to participants. Regardless of how much you have tested before, test everything again the week and day before your presentation. You certainly don't want to find out on the day of your presentation that URLs have changed or that your handouts do not contain updated information.

The goal of this first section, "Introduction to Virtual Presentations," was to provide you with a solid introduction to conducting knock-your-socks-off virtual presentations. Part 1 described virtual presentations and their benefits. It also identified the differences between virtual and face-to-face presentations, as well as when to consider virtual presentations and when not to. This first section also offered examples of how businesses are using virtual presentations and discussed the benefits of these presentations, the challenges involved, and how to meet those challenges. Finally, Part 1 concluded by revealing what you need to do to conduct virtual presentations that move people and drive them into action.

Part 2, "Making Effective Virtual Presentations," will cover the details of how to deliver outstanding virtual presentations. It will explore each element from preparing to evaluating your virtual presentations, as well as a few special chapters on elements that will make your virtual presentations sing.

MAKING EFFECTIVE VIRTUAL PRESENTATIONS

In order for any presentation, virtual or otherwise, to be successful, it should include several elements. In this portion of the book, we will present each of these elements, compare strategies for preparing for and conducting face-to-face and virtual presentations, provide you with a wealth of practical hints, and offer you at least one real-world example.

This section of the book contains the following chapters:

Chapter 11: Preparation and Administration: One Month before the Presentation

Chapter 12: Preparation and Administration: One Week before the Presentation

PREPARATION AND ADMINISTRATION: ONE MONTH BEFORE THE PRESENTATION

Meticulous preparation is even more important in planning a virtual presentation than in planning a face-to-face presentation. If you truly want to succeed, it is best to begin planning at least 30 days in advance, particularly if you will have more than 100 attendees. Complications tend to rise in accordance with the number of attendees, and there is a long list of tasks that you may need to complete even if you are presenting to a small audience. In many cases, you will need to collaborate with other people and organizations within your company, and the more quickly you reach out to them, the better.

COMPARING VIRTUAL AND FACE-TO-FACE PREPARATION STRATEGIES

Traditional Presentations

While each company and department is different, the most popular way to schedule meetings and presentations in advance is with Microsoft Outlook, unless your company has its own internal scheduling system. A month before the big day, you should begin developing your presentation or reviewing your existing presentation materials and customizing them for your upcoming session. Within this monthlong preparation period, you need to figure out what tools you will be using, and then, if you are not already proficient in their use, you need to become familiar with all of the hardware and software that you will use in conducting the presentation. It's always a good idea to print out the appropriate quantities of materials days in advance so that you do not have to scramble to get them printed at the last minute. Finally, a few days prior to the presentation, it's important to confirm participant attendance and send attendees a reminder e-mail.

Virtual Presentations

Scheduling and preparing to conduct a virtual presentation is similar to scheduling and preparing to conduct a face-to-face presentation. However, in the case of a virtual presentation, you will have a bit more to do, but you will have a more powerful and integrated system to help you. As in face-to-face presentations, you should use the virtual presentation software to send invitations, confirm participant registrations, and send reminder e-mails. A month prior to a virtual presentation, you will want to either create or review and customize the presentation materials, just as you would for a face-to-face presentation. Since the participants' attention may tend to wander more in a virtual meeting than in the face-to-face version, we recommend that you break up the presentation into sections that are 90 minutes or less in length. The main difference, preparation-wise, is that instead of making hard copies of your meeting materials, you will either upload them into shared folders in your virtual presentation software or distribute them electronically during your event. We also recommend that you make critical information (e.g., job aids) printable as Adobe documents.

ONE MONTH PRIOR TO THE PRESENTATION

Preparing for a small virtual presentation is simpler than preparing for a large one and can often be completed within a couple of days. On the other hand, preparing for a large virtual presentation with perhaps hundreds of attendees is a major undertaking. It involves managing the process; planning your presentation; preparing yourself and the other presenters; promoting the presentation; ensuring that you have appropriate personnel, facilities, and technology; collaborating with other departments; and communicating with attendees.

Managing It All

Arranging, preparing, and conducting a large virtual presentation requires the flawless execution of a multitude of activities. Probably the most important of these activities is selecting the people who will help you pull it all together and supervising them in performing their roles and responsibilities. As talented as you may be, you simply cannot perform all of these tasks alone. Conducting a large virtual presentation requires a wide variety of skill sets. And you know the old saying: the jack-of-all-trades is master of none. Table 11.1 identifies the types of help that you may need and their respective responsibilities.

Since the success of your presentation may not be the foremost priority for many of the people on your team, the iron hand in the velvet glove approach may work best. For smaller virtual presentations, one person may perform several if not all of the roles mentioned in Table 11.1. In any case, coordinating a virtual presentation is a lot of work. As with any other complex project involving multiple resources, developing and deploying

TABLE 11.1 ROLES AND RESPONSIBILITIES OF VIRTUAL PRESENTATION PERSONNEL

Role	Responsibility
Event coordinator	Schedules the event, manages setup in the virtual presentation service or application, and coordinates with other team members to ensure that deadlines are met
Marketing department	Promotes the event and drives attendance
Presenters	Deliver the virtual presentation
Producer/moderator	Supports the presenters with introductions, technical support, facilitating questions and answers, recording, and other on-air tasks
Business partners	Provide information and arrange for speakers, if necessary
Information technology department	Arranges, tests, and supports the virtual presentation application and software
Sales department (if the presentation is a sales presentation)	Provides sales leads, supplies information, reviews presentation, works with marketing in promoting the presentation, follows up promptly with leads, and continues to stay in contact to turn leads into prospects and customers

a virtual presentation should start with a project plan. Remember, those who fail to plan, plan to fail.

See Appendix B for a sample of a comprehensive virtual presentation preparation form that you can use to develop your project plan.

Scheduling Your Presentation

Consider the location of the audience members when scheduling your presentations. Are your attendees in the same city? Are they in the same state? Consider multiple time zones when you select the hour of your presentation, and make sure that everyone will be available at the time you schedule. Rotate meeting times if you are organizing regularly scheduled presentations that include people internationally. That way, no one has to get up early or stay up late every time.

In terms of dates, it is best to avoid holidays and the days immediately preceding them. A lot of people will be out of the office on vacation, and they won't be open to remotely tuning in to your virtual presentation. Also, if at all possible, avoid Mondays and Fridays, which have lower attendance on average. While it is difficult to generalize, many people either get off to a slow start on Mondays or want to complete the important activities that they have been worrying about all weekend. On the other hand, Fridays are the days when they want to complete their assignments and get an early start on the weekend. Avoid days that your audience is generally unavailable, such as the end of the month for sales or finance departments or the days prior to major corporate events for marketing departments.

Once you have your date down, select a time. In North America, 10:00 a.m. Pacific/1:00 p.m. Eastern Time generally gets the best attendance. I imagine that these times work because they are convenient for business professionals in multiple time zones. Between 10 a.m. and 4 p.m. Eastern Time in the middle of the week also works well, perhaps because this time frame allows attendees in that time zone to complete their important activities in the couple of hours at the beginning and end of the day. If you will be conducting a virtual presentation for consumers, 7 p.m. provides good attendance, and weekends do not.

Preparing Your Presentation

Hook Them in before You Even Begin

Create a media-rich and compelling self-running presentation to snag participants and keep them waiting until you begin your virtual presentation.

Timing Is Everything

Timing your virtual presentation is one of the most important preparation activities. Marketing and general informational Webinars should have a maximum length of 60 minutes. Training and educational Webinars can go as long as 90 minutes. For a 60-minute presentation, a possible scenario is to begin 2 minutes after the hour to allow for late arrivals. After that, the producer/moderator should spend 1 minute introducing attendees to the virtual conferencing controls and describing how they can interact and provide feedback. Then the presenter should conduct the presentation for 20 minutes, followed by 2 minutes for an audience poll. If the presentation has a second speaker, she should be introduced at this point and conduct a demonstration for 20 minutes. There should then be 13 minutes or so of interactive audience activity to keep the audience members engaged and help them apply the information that they have gleaned from the presentations, and finally the presenters should spend 2 minutes on closing remarks and action items. The actual model timing plan that you end up using will be based on the level of audience participation, the number of speakers, and how much information there is to disseminate. Make sure that each presenter and moderator has a copy of the timing sheet to ensure that each knows the amount of time he has to deliver his message. As I've said already, rehearsal is the key to a smooth presentation that finishes on time.

Preparing Yourself and the Other Presenters

Ensure that You Are Not the Weakest Link

When rehearsing, you should do both solo attempts and dry runs that include all the presenters and your producer/moderator. Even if you plan on using a producer/moderator, you should be competent at using the virtual presentation service or application that you will be employing; it is critical that you take the time to be trained to proficiency. Practice making virtual presentations to anyone who will help you, even if that means gathering a few associates during lunch break one day and asking them to sit through a shortened version of your presentation.

Be sure to get comfortable with not being able to make eye contact or to see the facial expressions or other forms of body language of your audience. You'll be surprised at what a difference it makes not being able to express yourself with your face and with your hand gestures. Learn to read audiences with the tools that you do have. Become adept at chatting, polling, and reading and responding to questions, because this feedback will prove invaluable to your presentation. Also spend some time using tools that support the other elements of your presentation so that you're familiar with everything. These may include audio and video players, groupware tools, or general software applications (e.g., Microsoft Excel). Leave nothing to chance!

Promoting Your Presentation

If a tree falls in the woods and no one is around to hear it, does it make a sound?

While the tree in that famous Zen Buddhist koan was completely soundless and thus poorly attended, you have the option of avoiding such an outcome for your presentation. Get the word out! Promoting your virtual presentation is serious business. Make sure that you spend the time needed and utilize the appropriate resources to help you publicize the presentation to all those who might attend. Here are a few ideas that I have come across for marketing your virtual presentation:

- Send attendees invitations at least two weeks prior to your presentation.

- For presentations that require more involvement, you may be enticed to send out comprehensive surveys for participants to complete or to ask them to complete some prepresentation work. My experience has been that most attendees do not want to do this, and if they do it at all, they complete these materials in the most cursory fashion. Be very sparing in what you ask for. Do not ask for more than a half hour's worth of thought, because if you do, you risk losing your audience before you presentation has even started. As an alternative, you can provide a few moments for attendees to complete these items during your presentation or while they are waiting for your presentation to begin.

- Create a presentation title and description that will intrigue your audience. Include a company logo. Most virtual presentation applications and services include invitation templates that you can customize. Pay attention to the quality of your invitation. Remember, you never get a second chance to make a first impression. Typos are deadly at this stage. Be sure to have someone else proofread your invitation. Avoid phrases that are blocked by spam filters, such as "free promotion" or "special offer." Finally, use a subject line that is short and descriptive and that will not be caught by spam filters. I recommend that you run some tests before you decide on your final choice.

- If you are asking attendees to register online, avoid the temptation to ask too many questions up front. If you do not need a fax number, do not ask for one. If you can get away with just a name and an e-mail address, good for you. Whatever you do, make potential attendees feel like valued guests instead of sales targets. Save the information gathering for a follow-up activity once they trust you.

- Remove any barriers and make the enrollment process quick and easy. Most virtual presentation applications and services have templates that you can use. Consider adding a short audio or video presentation compelling participants to attend your event.

- Make sure that you send a confirmation e-mail. The confirmation e-mail should contain a restatement of the value of the presentation and instructions for attending the presentation. Also, tell participants to expect some additional and valuable communication as the date of the presentation moves closer.

- The best-attended virtual presentations cover a very specific topic, are free, and are conducted by a presenter whom the audience is familiar with.

- For those of you who are using virtual presentations to drive sales, the attendance rates using standard business lists are low. With such lists, 30,000 to 60,000 invitations are typically required to achieve 100 attendees. Try your in-house list or lists generated by an association (e.g., American Medical Association) or industry group (e.g., National Association of Manufacturers).

Ensuring Appropriate Personnel, Facilities, and Technology

The "Right" People
Determine whether you will have multiple speakers and who those speakers will be. Later in this book, we give you some ideas for finding the right people. Explore your speaker's availability as soon as possible.

The "Right" Place
Arrange for a meeting room and appropriate technical equipment. We go into detail on this topic in a later chapter, but here is an overview. At a minimum, each presenter will need a space that is free of distraction. Each will also need a properly configured computer, virtual meeting software (if necessary), a quick and robust Internet connection, and a high-quality telephone or USB headset. All presenters can be in the same room or in different locations.

Technology That "Works"
Determine whether you will be using the telephone or the computer to provide audio support. I personally favor using the telephone, because if I use the computer, I will have a single point of failure. If something happens to my computer connection, I am in big trouble. I like to spread my risk over more than one technology. Computer audio or Internet telephone (e.g., Vonage) is better than ever, but it still has some risks. It is also not very friendly with firewall technologies.

Be sure to develop a contingency plan in case the technology malfunctions, such as the method that attendees should use to tell you that they have a technical issue. Consider providing them with your contact info, or your producer/moderator's. This way, attendees can reach one of you if your office lines are tied up by the virtual presentation. If you are considering recording your presentation, find out where you can store the recording so that attendees and other audiences can conveniently retrieve it.

Collaborating with Other Departments

WORK WITH YOUR INFORMATION TECHNOLOGY DEPARTMENT

Ensure, verify, and test that both the presenters and the attendees have the bandwidth, software, and other system resources required to successfully participate in the presentation. If necessary, redesign your presentation to conform to the attendees' limits as best as you can. Be sure to test your ability to send files through corporate firewalls and to access your media directly or view the media using screen sharing without significant delays.

WORK WITH YOUR SALES AND MARKETING DEPARTMENTS

If you are conducting a sales presentation, coordinate with your sales department to support each other's efforts in terms of generating sales leads, registration, updating materials, providing collaterals, and conducting the virtual presentation. Collaborate to create an integrated plan that includes follow-ups and a calling campaign by your sales force to qualified attendees. Determine a budget, identify resources, and plan accordingly. Be realistic. Most folks have a day job in addition to helping you. Should you be sending out marketing information or sales collateral at the conclusion of your presentation, make sure that the materials will be completed on time and be ready to go.

It's easier than you think to create a promotion plan that drives traffic to your presentation using home page placements and articles in your company newsletter. Utilize the resources that you already have at your disposal. Use company social networking groups or your department's electronic newsletter. Concentrate on emphasizing not the information that you will present, but why attending the event will add value to people's personal and professional lives. Make sure that all vehicles drive personnel to the registration form. There are ways to make even this aspect of your presentation seem creative. For instance, you can make the invitation look like a ticket. Avoid being too cutesy and including extraneous information, but otherwise have fun with it!

WORK WITH OTHER DEPARTMENTS

Contact the group that is responsible for providing you with a list of attendees. Make sure you have complete information, such as each person's name, title, affiliation, e-mail address, and phone number. If you cannot get the information at this time, arrange to receive such a list and identify when you will receive updates closer to your presentation. Another area where you may need to interact with a department that we have not mentioned is payment processing if you are charging people to attend your presentation. As of this date, few virtual presentation products have payment processing capabilities. Consider using services such as Eventbrite. Give some thought to how you will handle requests for refunds.

Communicating with Attendees

SEND ATTENDEES A CONFIRMATION E-MAIL

This note should identify the hardware (e.g., headsets) and software (e.g., the newest version of Adobe Acrobat) that people may need during the presentation and the level of computer proficiency required. Ask the attendees to download the necessary software and test the application before the day of your virtual presentation. You may wish to remind them of this the day before the presentation.

Now that we've taken a look at what you need to do for your virtual presentation way in advance of the deadline, let's see what kind of actions you can take one week beforehand.

PREPARATION AND ADMINISTRATION: ONE WEEK BEFORE THE PRESENTATION

t is just a week before your virtual presentation, and you want to make sure that everything goes just right. Here are some items that you want to make sure you have on your checklist.

SEND A MOTIVATING E-MAIL REMINDER TO PARTICIPANTS PRIOR TO THE PRESENTATION

Keeping your future attendees aware of the event will help to build excitement for it. If applicable, remind participants why the presentation is valuable to them personally, not just to their organization. Ideally, you want the attendees to feel as though they *get to* participate in your virtual presentation, rather than that they *have to* do so. Playing up what they

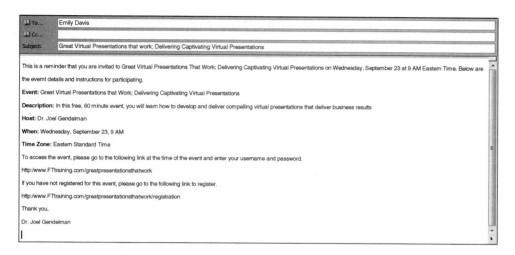

FIGURE 12.1: E-MAIL REMINDER

stand to benefit from it personally only increases your chance of this outcome. Be sure that your requests highlight what would be of value to them, not to you. To further hammer home this point, you might also ask attendees to note what they would like to cover, challenges they are experiencing, or their specific business goals.

This announcement should be more detailed than the confirmation. It should further identify the value of the presentation and include instructions for preparing for and participating in the event. Include help-desk information for technical problems that may occur before or during the virtual presentation. Warn participants not to plan to call from a cell phone. Often the reception is poor, and everyone gets to hear the static. Finally, recommend that audience members participate in the presentation using a headset or a quiet room, so that they can concentrate and not disturb others. Figure 12.1 is a sample of such a reminder.

REVIEW AND REFINE YOUR PRESENTATION MATERIALS

If you have conducted the virtual presentation before, take some time to refine the presentation based upon your prior experiences and to personalize the presentation to the attendees. Include their company logo in your presentation and handouts. Use terms that are part of their industry jargon. Incorporate the names of their products. Pepper your presentations with examples from their type of service.

CHECK THE ROOM WHERE YOU WILL BE CONDUCTING THE EVENT

If possible, gain information on the rooms that the attendees will use. If several participants are located at the same remote site, check that the site meets your needs in terms of the size and layout, access to computers, number of chairs, and equipment in working order. Ensure that the ventilation, temperature, lighting, noise level, and seating arrangements will not be distracting.

As the presenter, you may use a conference room, a corporate office, or your home office. You just want to make sure that you have a quiet and private location to eliminate distractions. If you will be conducting your virtual presentation from a home office, place the dog outside and ask your family to go to the mall or a park. Think about what is behind you. Strive for a neutral background.

SELECT YOUR WARDROBE

Lean toward the conservative side. You can always make your outfit more casual by removing your jacket, but you can't produce a jacket out of thin air, if it seems that you need one. Wear neutral, solid clothing. Avoid stripes, plaids, and floral designs. Make sure that your clothes contrast with the background colors. Try everything on beforehand to ensure that you have not gained enough weight to make for a distractingly too-tight outfit. This is the time to learn that a shirt is missing a button or that you need to take a trip to the dry cleaner, not in the middle of your presentation.

CREATE A LIST OF PARTICIPANTS

Include participants' basic job information, and distribute the list to all attendees. This will provide attendees with a sense of community and you with a vehicle for referring to participants by name and knowing something about them. Add more information about attendees as they introduce themselves, such as their company, department, position, and what they hope to glean from the presentation. In addition, maintain participant passwords and other access requirements.

UPLOAD SUPPORTING MATERIALS

If your virtual presentation software supports uploading materials to a shared folder, upload everything that you intend to distribute during the session to that folder. Then you won't have to worry about whether participants will be able to access the materials easily before, during, and after your presentation.

REHEARSE!

There is no substitute for rehearsal time. Each speaker needs to practice delivering her presentation aloud as if there were an audience listening. Rehearsing is the only way to work out timing, find the right words, and become comfortable with transitions and segues between talking points. As I've said before, audiences can easily distinguish between a presenter who is confident, unrushed, and unflustered and one who is struggling with phrasing and pacing. When you rehearse, practice slowing down your speech. Most presenters tend to move too quickly and risk breezing by a key point. When you rehearse, do so using the computer that you will use for the presentation. That way, you will be able to recognize and resolve issues way ahead of time.

PREPARATION AND ADMINISTRATION: ONE DAY BEFORE THE PRESENTATION

Since you have prepared meticulously for your virtual presentation both a month and a week before, you should be well on your way to success. The day before your presentation, you want to make sure that all the t's are crossed and the i's dotted. Here are some items that you want to include in your hit list.

CONDUCT A DRY RUN OF YOUR PRESENTATION

Include everyone who will be presenting during your virtual presentation, so that your dress rehearsal closely resembles your final product. Use all the tools and software that you will be utilizing for your actual presentation—that way, you will be forced to work out any possible last-minute technical glitches. Whatever would have come up on the day of the presentation will instead come up the day before. I find that the more you practice, the more spontaneous you can be during your presentation, because everyone will have his content and presentation strategy down tight.

DOUBLE-CHECK EVERYTHING TECHNICAL

Verify that all applications, Web links, and media presentations are working as expected. Ensure that all participants have access to the prepared resources and that the virtual meeting area is up and running. Confirm the readiness of participants' equipment and the resources used during the presentation (e.g., Web cameras, microphones, and access to online resources). Ensure that all presenter and attendee materials, such as presentation media, participant materials, and presenter materials (e.g., polling questions), are loaded or in a separate folder ready to use or be transmitted. Log on as a participant to ensure that attendees will be viewing what you expect them to view. Leave no room for chance in the form of technical glitches. It's like that old saying, "Fortune favors the well prepared."

SEND ANOTHER E-MAIL REMINDER

Once again, remember to focus clearly on the value of your presentation to attendees. Most people will have long forgotten the wonderful marketing points that you made in your previous communication. Your goal here is to reestablish the idea that your event is worth their time as they are trying to clear out tomorrow's calendar so that they can get some real work done. Restate the key activities that they need to perform in order to ensure a successful experience in your virtual presentation, as well as any major cautions (e.g., never place your phone on mute, disable call waiting) that they need to address.

CLEANSE BROWSER ENTRIES

Look at your automatic browser entries. Most browsers display the links that you have used before, and you may prefer that these not be public knowledge. They may represent your arcane personal interests, such as pets, dancing, and jokes. Personally, mine include http://www.mastiffrescue.org/main.htm, http://www.lindyexchange.com/site/future.aspx, and http://oldjewstellingjokes.com/. Some browsers allow you to delete these automatic entries, and others do not. Consider having a browser that you use only for your virtual presentations.

SET AN APPROPRIATE SCREEN SIZE

Not everyone has a large display. Either adjust your resolution to a reasonable 1,280 × 768 or shrink your application window. This will maintain the audience's focus, and the attendees will not see all your mail, messages, and alerts popping up.

PREPARATION AND ADMINISTRATION: THE DAY OF THE PRESENTATION

Today is the day, and if you have followed the guidelines in the last few chapters, you should be good to go. You just need to prepare yourself mentally and do some last-minute checking, and you are set to conduct a fabulous virtual presentation.

THE MORNING OF THE PRESENTATION

- **Keep calm.** As best as you can, avoid stress before your presentation. Steer clear of serious conversations or controversy with your kids. If you are commuting, leave a bit early to make sure that you are not rushed and have time to settle in once you get to the office.

- **Last call.** On the day of your virtual presentation, you will want to send one short final e-mail reminder to your participants. People are busy these days and often forget appointments and meetings. It's better to err on the side of peskiness than to be so concerned about not annoying people that you increase the chance that they will forget about your event. Last-minute reminders help. For sales presentations, call or have your sales department call attendees.

- **Test everything again.** So you have tested all your equipment within the week. That's excellent! However, there is always a chance that something could have happened during the course of the week. It's best to do one final check to make sure that everything is working as it should. This includes your Internet connection, virtual meeting service or application, presentation, media, materials you would like to share, and Web links.

- **Take care of your voice.** Avoid dairy products, caffeine, and smoking the morning of your presentation. This will prevent your need to repeatedly clear your throat or cough. It will also help you avoid that speedy feeling that may entice you to speak more quickly than you should.

AN HOUR BEFORE THE PRESENTATION

Send a final e-mail reminder. Gather your materials. Begin the media-rich and compelling autoplay presentation that you have prepared to snag participants and keep them waiting until you arrive. Log on as a participant, as well as a presenter, so that you can see what your attendees are seeing. Turn off cell phones and mobile devices so that they do not distract you in the middle of a sentence. Mute your computer sound, and shut down applications such as e-mail and instant messaging that could pop up a distracting message while you are trying to concentrate on your delivery. Keep a glass of liquid, at room temperature, handy to combat dry mouth. In addition, if you have two telephone lines, make sure that the second line does not ring during your presentation. Have all presenters close applications that they will not be using during your presentation and disable pop-ups. Place and adjust your headsets. You are now ready to go.

IMMEDIATELY PRIOR TO YOUR PRESENTATION

Begin your pre-presentation routine to get yourself into show mode. If you are already a seasoned presenter, you will know just what I mean. Arrive at the area where you will be conducting your presentation at least 30 minutes early. Start your presentation 15 minutes early and greet each attendee by name as he and she log in. Use audio or polling to ask the attendees a few prepared questions about themselves and how they hope to benefit from your virtual presentation.

PREPARATION AND ADMINISTRATION: DURING THE PRESENTATION

THIS IS YOUR TIME TO SHINE

You made it! The hard part is over—since you have rehearsed so much, the presentation should be a breeze. Remember to breathe and breathe deeply. Consider using an attention meter—similar to the "applause-o-meter" on old TV game shows—to let attendees continuously provide you with feedback on how interested they are in what you are saying and when they feel it is time for you to move forward. When you use screen sharing, ask attendees to let you know when they begin seeing your screen and if they are experiencing delays in watching media presentations.

MAKE TECHNICAL FACTS MORE INTERESTING

Technical facts need some smoothing over to make sure that they go down easily. Here are a couple of ideas for how to do just that.

Interactive Diagrams

Use the AutoShapes function of Microsoft Word or PowerPoint or Microsoft Visio to create graphic elements of a flowchart or process diagram. Employ these elements in presenting information. Better yet, encourage attendees to use these shapes in group and individual exercises to develop and share their own diagrams. This will add a wonderful visual dimension to your virtual technical presentations.

Technobabble Exercises

Make memorizing technical facts more relevant and interesting by concluding a technical presentation with a technobabble exercise. Separate attendees into pairs and place each pair in a separate breakout room. Assign one member of each pair the role of a "technically oriented" customer and the other the role of one of your company's sales personnel. The customer's job is to trip up the salesperson by slinging all the "technobabble" (e.g., names, abbreviations, and acronyms) she can to throw her opponent off base. The salesperson's job is to use his knowledge and a handout to translate what the customer said and not be thrown off the track.

LEAVE NOBODY BEHIND

Avoid scrolling quickly—some people take longer to read and digest information than others. Be aware that it may take a while for attendees' screens to refresh. Assume a couple of seconds of lag time so that you leave nobody behind. When it's important that the audience notices a particular point, pause, verbally call attention to what you would like the attendees to notice, and ask them if they are seeing it. If you click on something, describe what you are clicking on. Be sure to speak slowly and clearly. Avoid statements such as "look over here" or "notice this." Instead, use statements such as "look at the second bullet on the screen" or "notice the arrow at the top left-hand corner of your display."

BE VERY CAREFUL BEFORE YOU PRESS
THE SEND BUTTON

Be sure that you are sending your message where you want it to go. Otherwise, you can embarrass yourself and offend others. You typically have the option of sending comments to another presenter, to a specific attendee, or to all participants. Check for typos as best you can, using the spell-check feature of your word processing application to create and check your comment and then just paste in into your message window.

MAINTAIN A HIGH LEVEL OF ENERGY
WHEN YOU SPEAK

Sustain a fast and lively pace that might seem just a bit faster than is comfortable for the average participant. Smile; even if the attendees do not see you, a smile always shines through. You'll find that people seem to be able to *hear* your smile. Vary your intonations. This includes your pitch, volume, and inflections. When you change the way you sound at times, it keeps listeners interested. Stay positive and enthusiastic. Avoid statements such as, "I hope this works." Use the singular "you" in your statements and questions. Instead of saying, "I wonder if anyone out there can answer this question," say something like, "I wonder if you know the answer to this question." Listeners should have the feeling that you are speaking directly to them. Use attendees' names as much as you can to add further personalization.

WHEN YOU ARE SPEAKING, REMEMBER
THESE FEW THINGS

Paint pictures with your words. Vary your intonations. This includes your pitch, volume, and inflections. Use attendees' names as much as you can.

BE FLEXIBLE, AGILE, AND INTELLECTUALLY NIMBLE

This is probably the one element that separates great virtual presenters from simply good ones.

IN CASE YOU DO NOT HAVE ENOUGH TO REMEMBER, HERE ARE A FEW MORE THOUGHTS

Where appropriate, include support information such as Web resources and an e-mail box for questions to subject matter experts (SMEs). Include an "I didn't know that" whiteboard where participants can write something new that they learned during the presentation and how they intend to use it. Expect that unexpected things will happen. Remember that you can broadcast the results of a poll as it is running or wait until it is winding down. I recommend waiting until it is winding down, so that attendees do not alter their answers to agree with the majority.

AVOID DISTRIBUTING ALL OF YOUR HANDOUTS AT THE BEGINNING OF YOUR PRESENTATION

Attendees often look ahead. Wait to distribute handouts until they are needed. It is acceptable to include contact information in your handouts, so that attendees can reach out to you if they need to. Be sure to make this information understated and tasteful. Send private messages to attendees complimenting their chats and other involvement in your virtual presentation. Also, send chat messages to participants whom you feel need a little extra help or encouragement.

IMMEDIATELY FOLLOWING YOUR PRESENTATION

- Say "**thank you.**" Regardless of the type of virtual presentation you conducted, send an e-mail to each attendee thanking her for attending and recognizing her contribution. Do this within the next 24 hours. Getting a brief message of gratitude will help cement the presentation in people's minds as an experience that they enjoyed.

- **Keep your promises.** Follow up on any unanswered attendee questions using e-mail, blogs, or an online forum. If you told attendees that you would distribute copies of the presentation, reference information, or other marketing materials, have those files ready before you begin your presentation. Then send the materials immediately after your presentation. The more quickly you fulfill your obligations, the more you will maximize the impact of your material.

- **Give them something useful.** Send attendees something useful that is related to the presentation, such as a practical job aid that has answers to their most important questions. Edit and post your presentation for attendees and those who were not able to attend your presentation. In most cases, you should be able to streamline the virtual presentation by 50 percent in the version that you post afterward by removing extraneous information. I also recommend that you make all of your handouts available online, since sent or downloaded attachments do not make it through some corporate firewalls. Consider promoting your next presentation by including a link to a short presentation or audio recording.

- **Do not forget about registrants who did not attend.** It's important that you contact anyone who didn't manage to attend your presentation. A failure to attend usually does not indicate disinterest in the topic—perhaps the person was ill or otherwise occupied at the time. If your presentation is something that he needs to know, then make it your business to inform him. And even if their attendance wasn't absolutely necessary, registrants who did not attend are still excellent prospects for viewing recordings or signing up for future virtual presentations. Consider sending them the same materials that you send to attendees, as well as a link to the recorded presentation. Let them know where they can register for the next presentation.

- **Time is money.** If your virtual presentation is a sales vehicle, have the sales department contact participants no more then 24 hours after your presentation. The literature on sales effectiveness is clear. Calling an hour after your presentation will yield great results. A call within the first 24 hours will still be effective. If your firm calls within a week, you will achieve middling results. A call after two weeks or more is of no value, and you may as well forget it.

- **You can learn a lot from surveys.** Send a survey to participants, or use a survey service (e.g., SurveyMonkey) to make sure that the attendees received what they expected from your presentation. This will demonstrate to them that you care and provide you with valuable information to refine your future presentations. Consider asking attendees how well you met their need for information, how comfortable they feel with their ability to act on the information that you presented, and any questions or issues that remain unclear. Take a few moments to make some detailed notes on what worked, what did not work, and what you may want to modify for future sessions.

- **Keep attendees involved.** You might want to ask them to visit your Web site for more information or to download a white paper. Not only will this make them that much more likely to attend your next event, but it will help drive traffic to your Web site and potentially increase word of mouth. Make sure that these resources incorporate an explicit call to action, and let people know why taking that action benefits them.

- **Has your presentation made a difference?** Prepare a report to your management demonstrating the value of your virtual presentation. Consider reporting more than just the number of attendees and how well they liked the presentation, such as what they intend to do as a result of your virtual presentation.

- **Now, we begin again.** Endings are just new beginnings, so after basking in the sun of your successful virtual presentation, use the participant feedback that you have received to begin planning the next one so that it is even better.

TAKE ACTION

Review the virtual presentation preparation form in Table 15.1. Appendix B of this book contains a copy of this form that you can refer to in the future. It contains an exhaustive list of activities that need to be completed for a major virtual presentation to at least 100 attendees. If your presentations are a bit smaller in scale, you may need to complete only a subset of these activities. Consider a virtual presentation that you are presenting or plan to present in the near future. Use a highlighter or pen to identify those activities that you feel you would need to complete.

TABLE 15.1 TAKE ACTION: VIRTUAL PRESENTATION PREPARATION FORM

Element	Activity	Resource	Due Date
Administration and preparation	**A month prior to the presentation**		
	Complete the virtual presentation preparation form.		
	Schedule the presentation.		
	Select team members and assign roles.		
	Finalize contracts with outside resources.		
	Select a title and write a description of your presentation.		

(*Continued*)

TABLE 15.1 (CONTINUED)

Element	Activity	Resource	Due Date
	Prepare the virtual presentation, autoplay, and associated materials.		
	Prepare all presenters.		
	Promote the presentation.		
	Ensure that the appropriate personnel, facilities, and technology are available.		
	Collaborate with other departments.		
	Create a registration page.		
	Communicate with attendees.		
	A week prior to the presentation		
	Send an e-mail reminder.		
	Review and refine your presentation materials.		
	Check the rooms.		
	Select your wardrobe.		
	Create or acquire a participant list.		
	Upload supporting materials.		
	Conduct solo and group rehearsals.		
	A day before the presentation		
	Send another e-mail reminder.		
	Conduct a dry run.		
	Verify all applications, Web links, and media.		
	Cleanse your automatic browser entries.		

(*Continued*)

TABLE 15.1 (CONTINUED)

Element	Activity	Resource	Due Date
	Select an appropriate screen size.		
	The day of the presentation		
	Keep things calm.		
	Send a short e-mail reminder.		
	Test everything again.		
	Take care of your voice.		
	An hour before the presentation		
	Send a final e-mail reminder.		
	Gather your materials.		
	Log on to your computer.		
	Log on to a second computer connected to a second line.		
	Begin your autoplay presentation.		
	Turn off cell phone, e-mail, instant messaging, and pop-ups.		
	Mute your computer.		
	Shut down unneeded applications.		
	Keep a glass of water at room temperature nearby.		
	Place and adjust your headset.		
	Immediately prior to the presentation		
	Begin your pre-presentation routine.		
	Arrive at your presentation site 30 minutes beforehand.		

(*Continued*)

TABLE 15.1 (CONTINUED)

Element	Activity	Resource	Due Date
	Log on to your presentation 15 minutes early		
	Great each attendee by name.		
	Ask questions to show that you are interested.		
	During your presentation		
	Breathe and breathe deeply.		
	Verbally call attention to things that you would like attendees to notice.		
	Speak slowly and clearly.		
	Be very careful before you press the Send button.		
	Maintain a high level of energy when you speak.		
	Be flexible, agile, and intellectually nimble.		
	Avoid distributing all of your handouts at the beginning of your presentation.		
	Immediately following your presentation		
	Send attendees a thank-you e-mail.		
	Distribute promised materials to attendees.		
	Edit and store your presentation.		
	Send materials to nonattending registrants.		
	Make sure your sales department follows up within 24 hours.		

(*Continued*)

TABLE 15.1 (CONTINUED)

Element	Activity	Resource	Due Date
	Send out a brief survey to attendees.		
	Provide attendees with reasons to return to your Web site or to a follow-on presentation.		
	Make enhancement notes for future presentations.		
	Prepare and present a report to your management.		

GAINING ATTENTION AND ESTABLISHING RELEVANCE

Before you can accomplish anything in a presentation, you need to gain the attention of your attendees. An audience that sees no benefit for itself in a presentation is much more likely to tune out that presentation, and so you need to address this concern in the first 30 seconds of your virtual presentation. When you demonstrate to the members of your audience how they will be directly affected by the content of your presentation, not only do you get their attention, but you establish the relevance of what you have to say. We sometimes refer to this as "What is in it for me?" or WIFM. In some cases, you can persuade participants of the relevance of your presentation through a provoking question or quote, a hard-to-believe statistics, a satirical cartoon, or a compelling newspaper article. Here is an example of how to address the WIFM factor, in both an in-person and a virtual presentation, by differentiating your presentation from anything that your audience has ever seen before.

COMPARING VIRTUAL AND FACE-TO-FACE STRATEGIES

Face-to-Face Presentation

Display a PowerPoint of a cartoon like the one in Figure 16.1. This figure was used in a new product introduction to a sales audience. Select a cartoon in the same vein that is relevant to your presentation.

For the new product introduction, conduct a flipchart discussion of how your audience members felt the last time they participated in a new product introduction meeting. Write down their responses on the flipchart as rapidly as they come, and with enthusiasm. Quickly make a transition to what would have made the situation better. This could be shorter and more relevant meeting or eLearning that people can complete while they are traveling. Then move toward what you can do during this presentation to give them just the information that they need if they are to get started and begin selling. One solution may be to provide them with the most important sales points now and follow up with more detailed information on the sales department Web site. Then offer a more advanced presentation immediately before the new product is available for customers to order.

Virtual Presentation

Display a PowerPoint of the same cartoon as the one in Figure 16.1, or one in a similar vein.

By now you are familiar with the theme of this book, which is that you can re-create just about any experience from a face-to-face presentation in

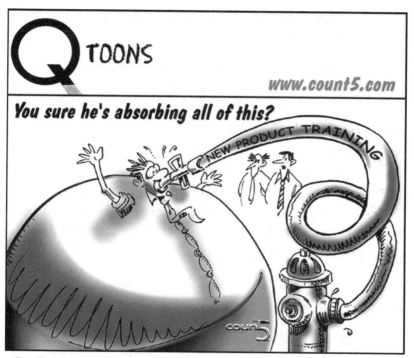

There IS a better way...and it's called "Q"

FIGURE 16.1: NEW PRODUCT TRAINING

Source: Used with permission from Count5 LLC.

a virtual presentation, and this is no exception. Once you display the cartoon on your audience's screens, ask the attendees to answer a series of questions regarding previous new product presentations. Instruct them to respond using the chat feature. Record their responses on the whiteboard, which you'll find works just as well as a flipchart. Use polling questions to determine the ideas that were most popular.

PRACTICAL HINTS

Here are some guidelines, hints, and ideas to consider in gaining your attendees' attention and establishing relevance in your virtual presentations.

Never Begin a Presentation by Having Attendees Introduce Themselves

Nothing is more boring at the beginning of a presentation than hearing an extended roll call. Instead, start out with a strong opening. Your introduction should showcase the relevance of your presentation. It should be scripted, memorized, and delivered with force. Remember, if you've rehearsed enough, it's easier to color outside of the lines by making some improvisational changes as you go along. Just don't stray too far from the script. Your introduction should capture the essence of your virtual presentation and grab the attention of the audience at the same time. A solid introduction will ensure that you start out strong and set the stage for building momentum as you continue.

Consider This Question

If you are looking for ways to make your presentation even more relevant to your audience, you may consider drawing people out by asking them directly what they would like to accomplish in the meeting. Their responses will help you focus your virtual presentation by letting you know which elements to play up.

Demonstrate That Your Presentation Will Be "Different"

As demonstrated with the cartoon example in Figure 16.1, it is important for the presenter to stand apart from other presentations that the audience has already seen. At the beginning of your presentation, demonstrate your interactive and casual style and your intention to be different. Within the first five minutes of your presentation, have your producer/moderator ask a planted and provoking question, one that you have prepared beforehand, such as, "How is this product different, and what makes it better than competitive offerings?" Then answer the question gracefully and honestly. Attendees generally will not ask questions until they see that it is safe to do so, and this will allay their fears.

Use More Than Just Words

Have attendees *experience* the importance of your topic. When you give a virtual presentation, you have all the multimedia that you'll ever need at your disposal. Wow your audience by deploying well-timed movie clips, audio, or cartoons to liven up and support your virtual presentation.

REAL-WORLD EXAMPLE 1

If your goal is to get your participants' attention in a meeting about, say, mastering a new technique for asking questions in consultative selling, begin by playing a media presentation demonstrating someone doing it really well. Then follow up with polling questions similar to these:

- Did the salesperson begin with an open-ended question?

- Did he ask more specific questions regarding the client's three-month, six-month, and one-year objectives?

- Did the salesperson determine the prospective client's buying criteria?

- Did he determine who else would be involved in the purchasing decision?

Ask attendees about their last major purchasing experience (e.g., a house or a car) and the types of questions that the salesperson asked them at the time. Request that they use the chat tool to send you a description of the situation, the questions that worked best, and those that did not work so well. Summarize these descriptions using the electronic whiteboard similar to the one shown in Figure 16.2.

Ask your producer/moderator to review the good and bad questions that attendees typed in the chat and select a few. Then conduct a poll asking participants to rank which questions they feel were the most in line with the consultative selling style (see Figure 16.3), and then ask for those that were the least in line with it. Be sure to use the whiteboard to

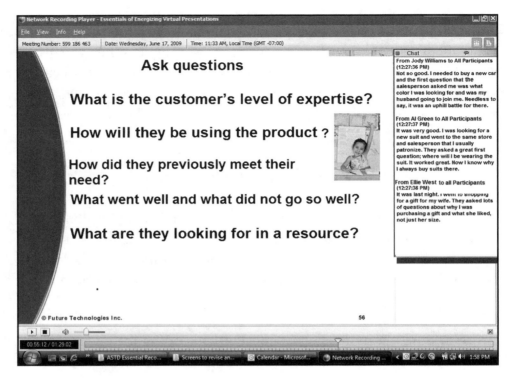

FIGURE 16.2: CONSULTATIVE SELLING 1: ELECTRONIC WHITEBOARD

highlight the importance of the consultative questioning technique that you just presented.

REAL-WORLD EXAMPLE 2

In covering "obtaining and using someone's last name in a sales or customer service situation," use the chat feature to pose a provoking question that challenges participants' belief on how often they use the names of people during routine conversations. Select a pair of attendees. Ask the first member of the pair to use the microphone to share something that happened to her today. Then ask the second attendee to question the first one about the specifics of the event. Throughout the exercise, ask the group to keep track of the number of times that

FIGURE 16.3: CONSULTATIVE SELLING: POLLING QUESTIONS

the second person used the first person's s name. Conduct a poll to summarize the results corresponding to the following questions (see Figure 16.4).

TRY IT YOURSELF

Now, try out some of the information that you covered in this chapter. Review the following situation. All you need to know is that your company, Starion, is a Fortune 1000 company and a premier manufacturer of mid-sized business equipment. It sells its equipment to large corporations through its direct sales force and to middle-market firms using established distributors that also sell other noncompeting products. Starion markets its products throughout the world.

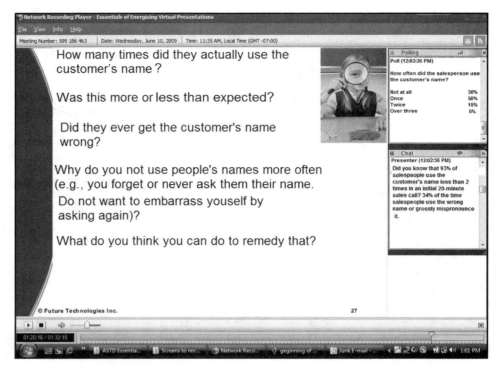

FIGURE 16.4: USING THE CUSTOMER'S NAME: POLLING QUESTIONS

The Situation

Starion is about to make a major worldwide product introduction. In three months, it will begin taking orders for the Transporter 1000. The Transporter is the size of a microwave and can digitize and transport a small package from one point to another anywhere in the world, instantly. The Transporter is a completely new product class that has no competition.

The company would like you to conduct a series of virtual presentations to introduce the Transporter 1000 to its 1,000 direct salespeople and its top 3,000 distributors and channel partners. The goal of this effort is to enable personnel to position the benefits and features of the product and demonstrate its compelling usefulness.

As is the case with most revolutionary products, selling the Transporter 1000 will have its challenges. Among them is the price. The price of each unit will be $50,000, and Starion has been unsuccessful in the past in selling equipment at that high a price point.

Starion would like you to lead this effort by collaborating with the sales, marketing, and IT departments. Your management expects you to be the major presenter, but to also include regional sales managers and senior product managers as additional presenters. It expects these virtual presentations to take between 60 and 90 minutes and to utilize portions of presentations that have already been prepared by marketing, as well as several planned collaterals and Web pages.

You have been chosen for this important assignment because of your reputation as a quick learner and a gifted presenter. You are honored, but you are a bit nervous. You are new to conducting virtual presentations, and you have never conducted one of this magnitude.

The Assignment

Use this information to plan a strong virtual presentation for Starion. Be sure to

- Capture the attention of the audience.

- Underscore the relevance of your presentation.

- Demonstrate your casual style and your intention to be different.

- Use stories, current events, cartoons, movies, newspaper articles, or television clips.

Some examples of compelling introductions and summaries are included in Appendix F. Take a moment now to review them.

Complete Table 16.1 to identify what you will do and script what you will say.

TABLE 16.1 TAKE ACTION FORM: GAINING ATTENTION AND ESTABLISHING RELEVANCE

	What You Will Do	What You Will Say (Script)
Capture the attention of the audience		
Underscore the relevance of your presentation		
Demonstrate your casual style and your intention to be different		
Use stories, current events, cartoons, movies, newspaper articles, or television clips		

INTRODUCING YOURSELF AND OTHERS

I n the previous chapter, we cautioned you against beginning your presentation by introducing yourself and asking attendees to introduce themselves. However, you still do need an introduction to establish your credibility to conduct your virtual presentations, and you would like to learn more about the particular group that you are addressing. Well, now is the time to introduce yourself and others.

COMPARING VIRTUAL AND FACE-TO-FACE STRATEGIES

Face-to-Face Presentation

On the back of an index card, ask each participant to note one fact about himself that no one would guess (e.g., flies Civil Air Patrol on weekends). Ask one person in each group to collect these cards and pass them to the front of the room. Then read off each experience, one by one, and ask the group to select the participant matching the card. Reveal the correct participant.

Virtual Presentation

You can use the same type of icebreakers and creative introductions in a virtual presentation that you would employ in a face-to-face presentation. For example, challenge participants to introduce themselves through the eyes of their pet. Ask attendees to display their picture or a picture of their pet. Just about everyone has a picture of herself or her pet stored somewhere on her computer. If someone doesn't, she can quickly go to the Web and find a picture of the same animal and breed as her family dog, cat, bird, or fish. You can also ask each participant to list on the electronic whiteboard something significant that she has experienced that few others would guess, as described in the face-to-face presentation example.

Enter a few of the most interesting of these replies on the electronic whiteboard (see Figure 17.1). After seeing photographs of each attendee, ask participants to type the name of a participant that they feel accomplished the unique activity next to each event. Then present the correct matches. Remember, in the beginning of your virtual presentation, you need to establish that this will not be just another boring presentation—that something different and engaging will be happening here. This is just one good way to accomplish this. As in any chapter in this book, use your imagination to derive a few ideas of your

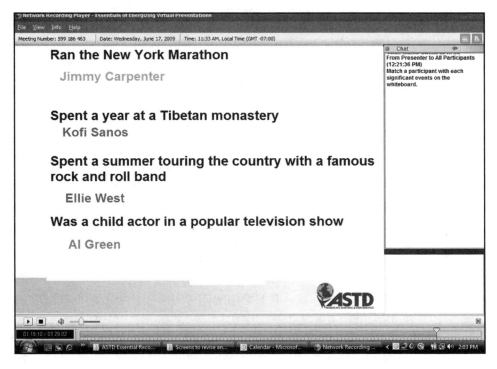

FIGURE 17.1: INTRODUCING ATTENDEES

own. We have included some more examples of virtual icebreakers in Appendix G.

PRACTICAL HINTS

Here are some guidelines, hints, and ideas to consider in introducing yourself and others.

- **Include contact information.** Be sure to display your e-mail address when you introduce yourself and encourage participants to contact you after the presentation if they have any questions.

- **Ask your producer/moderator to introduce you.** Having your producer/moderator introduce you adds to your professional allure. Since I am a modest person, I typically ask the producer/moderator to introduce me using a scripted introduction that characterizes me as larger than life. This introduction should be short and should clearly identify your credibility and expertise. You will want to mention your title and position, the company you work for, and your field of specialization. However, you may also wish to include relevant projects and accomplishments, positions of authority in professional associations, publications, and any awards you may have garnered. Be sure to thank the producer/moderator for his introduction when he is finished. From then on, having promoted yourself well, you can go back to being the modest person that you really are.

- **Use innovative methods for introducing participants.** It creates a great impression when you use innovative methods for gathering and sharing a participant's background information, as in the example demonstrated earlier. You can use your picture and pictures of participants to establish a human element in the presentation. Request that participants share background information, including their professional and personal interests and hobbies. Encourage attendees to use the whiteboard to highlight what is most important. But however you handle introductions, keep them short. This section of the presentation should take no longer than five minutes.

- **Seek and ye shall find.** Use polling to find out information about attendees that you think will prove helpful in conducting your presentation. This should include how familiar they are with your virtual presentation tools, their prior knowledge of the subject you are presenting, and any feelings they may have concerning the topic.

- **Review the basics.** Use the chat feature to share audio-conferencing details and other instructions that attendees need if they are to participate effectively in your virtual presentation.

TRY IT YOURSELF

Review the following situation, which is the same as the one that you worked with in Chapter 16.

The Situation

Starion is about to make a major worldwide product introduction. In three months, it will begin taking orders for the Transporter 1000. The Transporter is the size of a microwave and can digitize and transport a small package from one point to another anywhere in the world, instantly. The Transporter is a completely new product class that has no competition.

The company would like you to conduct a series of virtual presentations to introduce the Transporter 1000 to its 1,000 direct salespeople and its top 3,000 distributors and channel partners. The goal of this effort is to enable personnel to position the benefits and features of the product and demonstrate its compelling usefulness.

As is the case with most revolutionary products, selling the Transporter 1000 will have its challenges. Among them is the price. The price of each unit will be $50,000, and Starion has been unsuccessful in the past in selling equipment at that high a price point.

Starion would like you to lead this effort by collaborating with the sales, marketing, and IT departments. Your management expects you to be the major presenter, but to also include regional sales managers and senior product managers as additional presenters. It expects that these virtual presentations to take between 60 and 90 minutes and to utilize portions of presentations that have already been prepared by marketing, as well as several planned collaterals and Web pages.

You have been chosen for this important assignment because of your reputation as a quick learner and a gifted presenter. You are honored, but you are a bit nervous. You are new to conducting virtual presentations, and you have never conducted one of this magnitude.

Your Turn

Take this opportunity to script an introduction that you would like your producer/moderator to use in introducing you if you were conducting the Starion presentation just described. Here is an introduction that I have scripted:

> Our presenter this afternoon is Howard Jenkins, the consummate high-technology salesperson. He began his career with Starion 20 years ago as a technician. Since then, he has risen quickly through the ranks as an account representative, district manager, regional manager of the Northeast Region, and finally vice president of sales. Howard also has spoken and published extensively, most recently the headline article in the May issue of *Selling Prowess*. Just last month, Howard was awarded an honorary MBA from Harvard and a Ph.D. in marketing from Stanford University. Without further ado or fanfare, I give you Howard.

In the following spaces, write an introduction for yourself. Remember to get into character and to script an introduction for yourself not as you are, but as a credible presenter of a virtual presentation introducing Starion's new Transporter 1000.

_____

_____

_____

_____

_____

_____

Create a plan for having your attendees introduce themselves to the other participants. This chapter presents a couple of unique strategies. Use one of these or try one of your own.

_____

_____

_____

_____

_____

_____

_____

_____

IDENTIFYING OBJECTIVES AND SETTING EXPECTATIONS

Attendees have a right to know what they can expect to get out of your virtual presentation, and you have a responsibility to tell them this clearly. Establishing goals and ground rules is important for any meeting, and a virtual presentation is no exception. It is extremely important to be respectful and to identify proper online etiquette at the beginning of a virtual presentation.

COMPARING VIRTUAL AND FACE-TO-FACE STRATEGIES

Face-to-Face Presentation

Key ground rules for face-to-face meetings include turning off cell phones, not sending or responding to e-mails, actively participating, paying attention, asking and answering questions, and treating colleagues respectfully. An example of an effective strategy includes the following:

- Conduct a flipchart discussion on the goals of the presentation.

- Distribute and present a handout covering the expectations for the presentation and identifying how they relate to the purpose of the meeting.

- Discuss the format of the presentation.

- Display its agenda.

- Ask participants if they have any questions.

Virtual Presentation

It's equally important, if not more so, to set the tone early in a virtual meeting. Since the presenter cannot see the attendees and they are already using their computers, the chances of their etiquette being less than stellar are pretty high. Unless you lay the groundwork, that is. Ground rules in a virtual presentation should cover the following:

- Do not call in from a cell phone because the chances of getting disconnected are greater.

- Do not use speakerphones or microphones—use a telephone or USB headset.

- Do not place this call on hold, and be sure to place the call on mute when you are not speaking.

- Disable call waiting and instant messaging and e-mail alerts.

- Close down all applications that will not be used during the virtual presentation.

- Be patient and do not speak on top of each other. Identify yourself when speaking, and always speak clearly.

- Reduce distractions (e.g., barking dogs or TVs in other rooms).

- Close your door.

- Avoid side conversations with colleagues.

- Do not send or respond to e-mails.

- Participate actively in chats and ask questions.

- Be courteous in chat entries, postings, and e-mails.

- Do not send private chat messages to other participants once the session starts.

An example of an effective strategy includes the following:

- Conduct the same type of discussion regarding the goals, format, and agenda of the presentation as you would in a face-to-face presentation.

- Conduct a discussion using the chat feature and summarize responses on the electronic whiteboard.

- Use the polling feature to verify participants' agreement with the ground rules and goals.

- Ask participants to download more detailed information from a shared document folder, or distribute the document electronically.

PRACTICAL HINTS

Here are a few practical hints to consider in identifying objectives and setting expectations.

- **Provide the objectives of the presentation without calling them objectives.** No one likes the term *objectives*. It makes a casual presentation sound like a stuffy training session, and that is not how you want to begin your exciting virtual presentation. Explain how achieving the goals of the presentation will be useful to attendees.

- **Share the format of the meeting (e.g., presentation, practice, or something else).** Display the virtual presentation schedule in the media window divided into small pieces, similar to a meeting agenda.

- **Ask your producer/moderator to demonstrate the basics of how to use the virtual meeting tools and provide attendees with some practice.** This should include how the attendees will be able to participate in the presentation and ask questions. It should cover the electronic whiteboard, polling, and chat tools. One idea is to conduct a game in which participants practice using their drawing tools to identify their location. The producer/moderator can also provide attendees with some practice with polling, using fanciful questions such as their favorite food, sport, movie, song, type of music, or dance. The producer/moderator should review how to use less frequently used tools immediately before attendees need to use these tools in your virtual presentation.

- **If your session is longer than one hour, plan for a break or interactive activity every 50 minutes.** Most people get restless after about an hour, and you would prefer attendees not to feel that they have to leave your presentation for a bio break.

- **Ask for audience feedback on how everything is working.** Before you get into the meat of your virtual presentation, ask if people can see the presentation and hear you.

- **Present the contingency plan in case the virtual meeting service or application fails.** Tell the attendees how you will contact them. Provide attendees with your telephone number and e-mail address, and also those of your producer/moderator.

REAL-WORLD EXAMPLE

As an example, you can use the following strategy to demonstrate the ground rules of the presentation.

Utilize the chat feature to ask the following questions (see Figure 18.1):

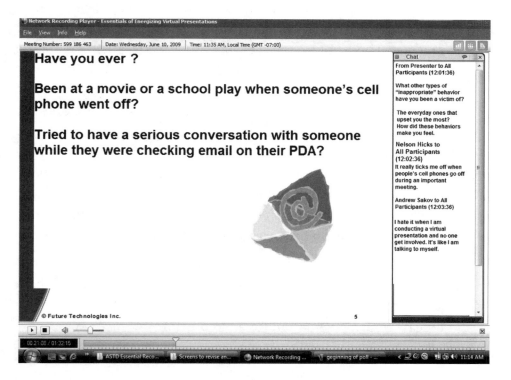

FIGURE 18.1: HAVE YOU EVER?

- Have you ever been at a movie or a school play when someone's cell phone went off?

- Have you ever tried to have a serious conversation with someone while she was checking e-mail on her PDA?

- What other types of disruptive behavior have you encountered in meetings or presentations?

- How did these behaviors affect your enjoyment of the event?

Facilitate a discussion and list behaviors that are unacceptable in virtual presentations on the electronic whiteboard (see Figure 18.2). These may include all the behaviors that we went over earlier in the chapter. Discuss this list with your participants using the chat feature.

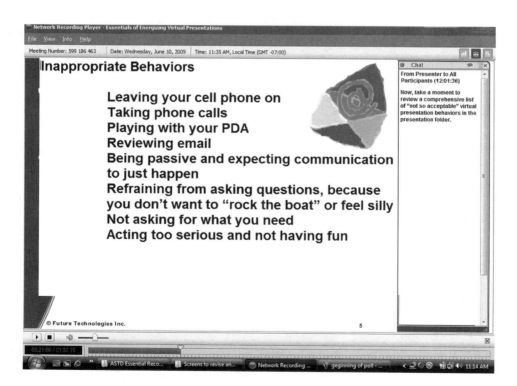

FIGURE 18.2: INAPPROPRIATE VIRTUAL PRESENTATION BEHAVIOR

TRY IT YOURSELF

Let us continue working on the presentation that you began in Chapter 16. How will you set your expectations for attendees in a nice, thorough, and direct manner? In Table 18.1, identify the actions, tools, and assets that you will use. I completed the first action, just to give you a running start. Now it's your turn—kindly finish the rest.

TABLE 18.1 TAKE ACTION FORM: SETTING EXPECTATIONS

Actions	Tools	Assets
Ask attendees specific questions about how they felt when a presentation they went to was disrupted.	Chat	Prepared question sheet stored in a shared folder.

PRESENTING INFORMATION

Presenters spend most of their time presenting. Unfortunately, the "presenting" part can be the most boring portion of any event; therefore, you should spend no more than 50 percent of your virtual presentation actually presenting. Some of you may have been born with, or have since developed, a unique skill in presenting information. Most people do not have this skill, however. If you do, consider yourself fortunate. Since this is a book on making presentations, I should clarify what I mean here. Strong presentations include a variety of communication elements. Actually presenting the information is only one of those elements. Other elements include demonstrating or conducting interactive activities.

Presenting can be especially toxic (i.e., boring) in virtual presentations, since time seems to go more slowly when participants lack physical contact with a group. Make your presentations as compact as you can. Try to economize by focusing on a few major points. If you are using PowerPoint slides, attempt to display a new one at least every three to five minutes. Supplement your presentations with demonstrations, question-and-answer sessions, and audience interaction. Finally, use a variety of content delivery types and media. And, of course, make use of relevant visuals whenever you can.

COMPARING VIRTUAL AND FACE-TO-FACE STRATEGIES

Face-to-Face Presentation

A big part of how you present information is with your finely honed speaking skills. Support your lecture by using slides, flipcharts, external media, and relevant Web sites. Whenever possible, use stories and analogies to illustrate a point. Pepper your presentations with questions, and draw out more seasoned participants to provide relevant examples. Consider using one or more formats of interactive lectures. Interactive lectures are those that actively involve attendees, instead of simply asking them to listen. One example of an interactive lecture is a question-and-answer lecture, where you place questions under the seats of selected participants and periodically request that attendees ask one of those questions to guide your lecture. *Thiagi's Interactive Lectures* (S. Thiagarajan, 2005) is an excellent resource for some great examples of interactive lectures.

Virtual Presentation

Introduce your presentation with a snappy prepared multimedia presentation that you have created using Adobe Captivate, Flash, or

Dreamweaver. If you are using supporting Web sites, direct attendees to them by sending the URLs in a chat. Solicit attendees' expertise, opinions, and thoughts by privately asking them to share stories, analogies, or other information using their chat or audio. You can also request that attendees utilize the electronic whiteboard and associated drawing tools to support or summarize their contribution. Then bring together the various threads of the presentation in a short discussion.

PRACTICAL HINTS

Here are some practical hints to consider in presenting information in your virtual presentation.

- **Never be the "sage on the stage." Always attempt to be the "guide on the side."** Unless you are a thrilling speaker or a Nobel Prize winner, or unless your audience is composed of young children, no one fully appreciates a sage. Attendees want to have some participation in the experience and some involvement in its direction. You are the presenter, though, and you are there for a reason. You were chosen because of your credibility and expertise. You have a great deal of wisdom and knowledge to share. That is not enough. A major factor in the success of your presentation will be your ability to relate to the members of your audience and get them involved in your presentation.

- **Everyone likes a good story.** Use case studies or stories to engage participants. Ask participants to share their own experiences related to the content. A good story is like the peanut butter with the pill inside—it makes everything go down more smoothly. When people are relating to you, they will be more open to the information that you present and whatever actions you suggest that they take.

- **Use strong presentation strategies.** Present key ideas using different types of media. These include text, graphics, animations, illustrations, diagrams, schematics, and models. Keep in mind that excessive animation can be distracting and that lengthy text is difficult to read on the screen. Use additional presentation strategies that include simulations, analogies, case studies, examples of doing it "right," nonexamples that showcase what *not* to do, mnemonics, jokes, war stories, and testimonials. The sky is the limit, and you are restricted only by your imagination. There are many different content delivery types (lectures, interviews with subject matter experts, participant demonstrations, and so on), and you should switch between them frequently. Tell stories to support your main points, and add interesting photographs and other media. Present information in a video format when you need to conduct a live demonstration or to include a message from senior management or other company leaders.

- This topic can be a book in and of itself. Try to learn from those who excel at presenting. You may or may not agree with the message of television evangelists, but you cannot deny that they are excellent at telling relevant stories. If these examples are not for you, listen to or read the speeches of great orators, such as the Reverend Dr. Martin Luther King, Jr., and Abraham Lincoln.

- **Present familiar information from another point of view.** If you are covering the history of England, do so from the perspective of King Arthur. Try acting out the role of the customer and presenting information from her standpoint on the efficient usage of the application you're presenting.

FOCUS ON THE DELIVERY, NOT JUST THE CONTENT

While the content of your presentation is crucial, the way you deliver it plays a huge role in how the audience accepts your message. Here are a few important guidelines to adhere to:

- **Stick to the schedule.** People often plan back-to-back meetings, so be sure that you begin your presentation on time, regardless of any stragglers. Even more important, end on time. To ensure that you end on time, do not review the beginning of the presentation for those who arrive late. While it may be okay for you to go over by 5 or 10 minutes, this usually is not convenient for most attendees, whether they say so or not. Keep your promise and end on time.

- **Structure your presentation for maximum impact.** Address the most important issues on the presentation outline first. That way, if you run over and need to cut some topics short, it will not be the important ones. Assess the group's progress throughout your presentation by posing questions, initiating polls, or simply asking people to tell you if they are "with you."

- **Present information in short and logical chunks.** Take care to sequence the information that you present using some logical method. Some standard methods of sequence are from the simple to the complex or from events that happen first to those that occur last.

- **Maintain a casual and effective tone.** Utilize a casual, yet respectful tone in postings, chats, stored standard responses, and e-mails. Except for the introduction and summary, never read from a script. Deliver the content naturally and with a smile. Even if you are on the phone, a smile usually shines through. Throughout the session, use changes of pitch, volume, and vocal expression to build enthusiasm for the topics you are presenting. Vary the range and volume of your voice by pausing to emphasize important points. Consider using emoticons. These are those symbols that many people use in text messages to express their emotions, such as :) for a smile or :(for a frown. You can often use emoticons to add a personal touch to your chats and e-mails. Appendix D contains a listing of common emoticons.

- **Keep a brisk pace.** The pace of a virtual presentation should always be brisk, but that does not mean that you always have to continue moving forward like a locomotive. Vary the pace and format of the presentation every five or six minutes. Learn to use the pregnant pause to let ideas dangle in the air, to provide attendees with an opportunity to process what has been said, or to highlight major thoughts. Using pregnant pauses is very much like tasteful musical phrasing: it keeps the ear from becoming bored, inserts some unpredictability into your presentation, and ensures that attendees' attention does not stray too far.

- **Presentations can be like symphonies.** You can get a lot of mileage out of simple repetition in a presentation. When used appropriately, a key phrase that you return to again and again will stick in the audience's thoughts like a mantra. Similarly, some of the most memorable musical pieces always return to the theme. Great virtual presentations always repeat key phases to focus the audience's attention on the major points and calls to action. One trick is to change where you place the accent for the sake of variety, but be sure to hammer your message home. Repetition is critical; it's how people remember. Stick to what is important, and say it again and again. It's easy to be repetitive in different ways, considering all the tools that a virtual presentation provides. You can introduce a topic in a multimedia presentation, then present it using the electronic whiteboard, and finally review the topic in a discussion using the chat or polling feature.

Artful usage of repetition is something that separates good presenting from great virtual presenting. Sometimes a rock-solid presentation will remind me of *Pictures at an Exhibition*, by Modest Mussorgsky. The piece is a musical walk through an art exhibition organized posthumously for a dear friend of the composer, Victor Hartman. Each movement of the piece is a musical description of one of the paintings in the exhibit. The main musical theme of the piece is a promenade that begins the piece and guides the listener from one picture to another. The promenade is always a bit different until it thunders into the final picture, "The Great Gate of Kiev." For those of you who have never heard the piece, go out and listen to it. It is a wonderful example of maintaining listeners' attention.

- **Roll with the punches.** If there are outside distractions as you are presenting, let participants know what is occurring. This will make them feel as if they are in the same room with you. Refrain from making any negative remarks, especially if you are using a recording device for your presentation. Do not show anger. Breathe when you feel yourself getting irritated. Write yourself a reminder note about not getting angry, and place it by your monitor.

USE YOUR TOOLS WELL

Use the electronic whiteboard as you would a flipchart to trigger visual memory. Point to, highlight, draw, and notate application screens. Enable participants to download documents from a shared folder. Be sure to use PDFs, as they display and print more predictably. Ask participants to refer to Web sites and other resources. Use them as valuable sources of information and activity material. If you want attendees to explore a Web site, type or paste the Web site's URL into a chat. That way, attendees can simply copy and paste it into their browser, instead of having to retype it.

- **When to speak and when to chat.** You should consider several factors in deciding whether you would prefer attendees to speak up during an activity or whether it would be better for them to send you their comments in a chat. Table 19.1 summarizes when you should consider each one.

- **Using a Webcam.** Although you do have the option of integrating a Webcam into your presentation, it is by no means a necessity. Plenty of people deliver top-notch virtual presentations without them. The motion is often choppy and not synchronized with the audio. Think about using a short multimedia presentation that

TABLE 19.1 WHEN TO SPEAK AND WHEN TO CHAT

When to Speak	When to Chat
Accomplishing your goals requires trust.	You expect a large number of attendees.
Attendees' remarks will typically be short.	Attendees' remarks may be long.
You can expect few distractions or can handle most of them by placing attendees on listen-only mode.	You would like to capture attendees' questions and comments electronically.

uses graphic visuals and a voice track. If you do use a Webcam, consider the following:

- Use a solid-color background if you intend to use a background.

- Place plants or flowers in the background to give your room a lived-in look and feel. If that is not possible, utilize a large sheet of colored cardboard on the wall.

- Dress appropriately. Select conservative clothing. You can always remove your jacket or open your collar if you feel that you have dressed too formally. Choose neutral colors, and avoid stripes, plaids, and floral designs. Make sure that your clothes contrast with the background colors.

- Sit up straight and lean slightly forward, but vary your position and posture at times for the sake of variety.

- Minimize your gestures. Slow transmission rates may make your gestures look like twitches.

- Let the camera see your eyes. Do not wear a hat or long bangs. If possible, do not wear glasses, or wear frameless ones with nonreflective lenses.

- Limit your accessories, especially if you have a tendency to fidget with them.

- **Again, test** *everything.* I can't stress this point enough: all the equipment must be tested repeatedly. Even after the virtual presentation starts, you can do one final test: assess the quality of audio and video transmission by polling participants to determine if everything is coming in clearly.

REAL-WORLD EXAMPLE

Following is an example from a virtual presentation identifying the elements of an effective greeting for customer support and service personnel. The steps given here identify the actions of the presenter of this virtual presentation in presenting information.

1. Initially use Figure 19.1 to illustrate the elements of an effective greeting.

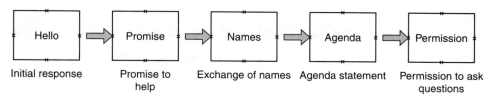

| Hello | Promise | Names | Agenda | Permission |

Initial response   Promise to help   Exchange of names   Agenda statement   Permission to ask questions

FIGURE 19.1: ELEMENTS OF AN EFFECTIVE GREETING

2. Next, use the chat and whiteboard capabilities to present the elements of a greeting (see Figure 19.2).

3. Finally, play media presentations of the effective usage of each element.

TRY IT YOURSELF

Use Table 19.2 to apply what you covered in this chapter to the presentation that you have been working on since Chapter 16. Review the material in this chapter, and clearly identify how you will accomplish several major guidelines in presenting information.

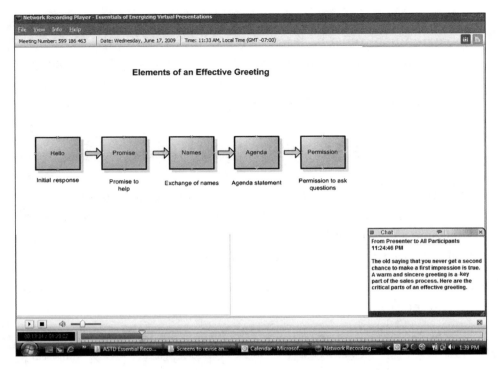

FIGURE 19.2: PRESENT THE ELEMENTS OF AN EFFECTIVE GREETING

TABLE 19.2 TAKE ACTION FORM: PRESENTING INFORMATION

Major Guideline	How You Will Accomplish It
Employing more diverse presentation strategies (which ones will you use?)	
Being the "guide on the side" instead of the "sage on the stage"	
Employing graphics (specifically, what graphics will you use?)	

(Continued)

TABLE 19.2 (CONTINUED)

Major Guideline	How You Will Accomplish It
Will you mostly be using your voice or the chat feature and why?	

The Situation

Starion is about to make a major worldwide product introduction. In three months, it will begin taking orders for the Transporter 1000. The Transporter is the size of a microwave and can digitize and transport a small package from one point to another anywhere in the world, instantly. The Transporter is a completely new product class that has no competition.

The company would like you to conduct a series of virtual presentations to introduce the Transporter 1000 to its 1,000 direct salespeople and its top 3,000 distributors and channel partners. The goal of this effort is to enable personnel to position the benefits and features of the product and demonstrate its compelling usefulness.

As is the case with most revolutionary products, selling the Transporter 1000 will have its challenges. Among them is the price. The price of each unit will be $50,000, and Starion has been unsuccessful in the past in selling equipment at that high a price point.

Starion would like you to lead this effort by collaborating with the sales, marketing, and IT departments. Your management expects you to be the major presenter, but to also include regional sales managers and senior product managers as additional presenters. It expects these virtual presentations to take between 60 and 90 minutes and to utilize portions of presentations that have already been prepared by marketing, as well as several planned collaterals and Web pages.

You have been chosen for this important assignment because of your reputation as a quick learner and a gifted presenter. You are honored, but you are a bit nervous. You are new to conducting virtual presentations, and you have never conducted one of this magnitude.

CONDUCTING DEMONSTRATIONS

The main point of almost every presentation, when it comes right down to it, is to show people things—for example, the features and benefits of a new product, how to use a new computer application, change a tire, or calm down an irate customer. Describing situations and presenting information take up the most time in a typical presentation, but aside from the informational aspect, presentations are supposed to be demonstrative. When they are not talking, seasoned presenters are typically conducting demonstrations or facilitating activities. Effective demonstrations do not happen by accident; they require diligent preparation, hard work, and, of course, lots of rehearsal.

COMPARING VIRTUAL AND FACE-TO-FACE STRATEGIES

Face-to-Face Presentations

Demonstrations are an important part of presentations. Demonstrations show attendees how something works or how to do things. While it's true that probably the best way for people to learn is by doing, if doing is not feasible in a particular learning situation, the next best thing is to watch someone else do it. Demonstrations can be live, or they can be recorded. Typically, demonstrations are used to show positive examples of whatever the subject of the presentation is. However, they may also include negative examples. After all, sometimes the lead-in is a faulty example that showcases what *not* to do.

In addition to modeling appropriate behavior, you may ask participants to demonstrate the action itself—the aforementioned learning by doing—and receive feedback from the presenter or their peers. As you will see in this chapter, a live demonstration can be carried out just as effectively in a virtual presentation as in a face-to-face one.

Virtual Presentations

Since the media window that displays your PowerPoint, video, photographs, and other media will typically be small, it is best to show only the most relevant portions of a demonstration. With your drawing and text tools, you have the ability to highlight and label the images that you choose to display on your screen, so that your attendees can easily focus on what is most salient.

You may display all of your computer screen or only a portion of it, such as only one application. This capability is particularly useful in demonstrating computer software. It enables you to focus on only the portion of your screen that is critical to that step of the process. Again, employ your drawing tools to label or highlight sections of the screen that you want attendees to focus on. You can also display participants' screens in the media window, instead of your own. This allows attendees to demonstrate "their" usage of applications or to share information as part of an interactive activity. In virtual presentations, both you and the members of your audience may use the whiteboard for visual support, which is particularly helpful for attendees when you are conducting demonstrations.

No matter how much you rehearse and prepare, there is, unfortunately, no guarantee that a demonstration will go according to plan. As in any mode or presentation medium, you need to be resilient and resourceful. If an activity that you have designed is not working, change it. If the medium is not functioning, use another one. Always have a backup plan.

PRACTICAL HINTS

There are seven rules when it comes to giving great virtual demonstrations, discussed in detail here.

1. **Make your demonstrations simple.** Good demonstrations are short, simple, and clearly focused. They typically cover the most salient points of a few important topics. Since they are direct and to the point, they capture and retain attendees' attention, rather than allowing it to wander.

2. **Keep your demonstrations real.** Incorporate case studies related to real-life situations and realistic problems. If you are demonstrating the use of a computer application, use slightly cleansed examples from your department (e.g., with customer and confidential information removed), using your screens, templates, and documents. Employing realistic examples increases the credibility of your presentation and ensures the relevance of your session.

3. **Make your demonstrations come alive.** Use photographs or media recordings of demonstrations whenever possible. Sure, it would

be great to have professionally developed media, but for most applications, less than broadcast quality will do. Software applications of varying levels of sophistication are available that will make this easier. Consider using tools such as Windows Movie Maker for simple video, Snagit for static screen shots, and Adobe Captivate for capturing computer sessions. Most of these applications have tools for editing, highlighting, incorporating audio, and annotating. Incorporating these elements into your demonstrations will provide them with the variety and richness that will make them jump off the screen.

4. **Ensure that your demonstrations are easy to follow.** People might understand what they are seeing, but miss its significance unless you explain it to them. Multiple presenters work very well for participating in and explaining demonstrations, as long as only one speaks at a time. If multiple presenters are talking over each other, the audience will not know where to focus its attention. Furthermore, it looks sloppy or amateurish.

   You can also use the drawing and text tools, as described earlier, for highlighting and labeling photographs or media presentations. Incorporate explicit instructions that direct participants to locations in a graphic or a photograph. Summarize these directions in a chat window when you feel it will be helpful. Separate complex demonstrations into smaller ones so that your audience can grasp the material more easily. Do not group all of your demonstrations together, one after the other. Instead, move back and forth between presentations and interactive activities so that the audience stays with you.

5. **The best demonstrations are visual.** Online screen sharing is a great way to demonstrate computer applications. Remember to use the drawing tools to label or highlight sections of the screen. Do not add text in your PowerPoint presentation that repeats what is in the audio. That is just repetitive and boring, and it diverts attendees' attention. Avoid PowerPoint slides that are filled with

text. Instead, use photographs or graphics with annotations for a visual flourish.

6. **Get your audience involved.** Ask members of the audience to "take over the reins" and conduct their own demonstrations. This is done by passing control of the application window over to them. The mechanics for passing control are different for each virtual meeting service and application, but in all cases, it's a simple process. Then use the whiteboard, chat, or audio to facilitate a discussion of the method that the participants used, what could have been done better, or what could have been done differently. If you wish to walk participants through a process or procedure in different situations, be lazy and let participants do some of the work. You may accomplish this by narrating a step and then involving participants by asking them to enter what they believe is the next step into the chat window. Avoid relying on demonstrations of the "right" way. It is okay to demonstrate the wrong, not-so-right, or just different way and ask the audience to make its own judgments and recommendations. You may find out that there are several very good ways to achieve the same result.

7. **Finally, do not forget to recognize participants for their contributions.** These days, you cannot expect or demand attendees' involvement. You need to earn it, be thankful for it, and express your appreciation of it.

REAL-WORLD EXAMPLES

Example 1: Conducting Effective Discovery

Here is an example from a virtual presentation on the steps in discovering customer needs and wants that utilizes the audio feature. These steps identify the actions of the presenter of this virtual presentation in conducting demonstrations.

1. Identify and demonstrate the steps in discovering customer needs and wants using the audio.

2. Summarize the elements of the technique using the electronic whiteboard (see Figure 20.1). The elements include the following.

   ○ Ask questions—Can you tell me more?

   ○ Restate—So, what you are saying is . . .

   ○ Empathize—I can understand that . . .

   ○ Uncover—In addition to that, is there anything else that concerns you?

   ○ Confirm—Of those things that you mentioned, which is the main issue?

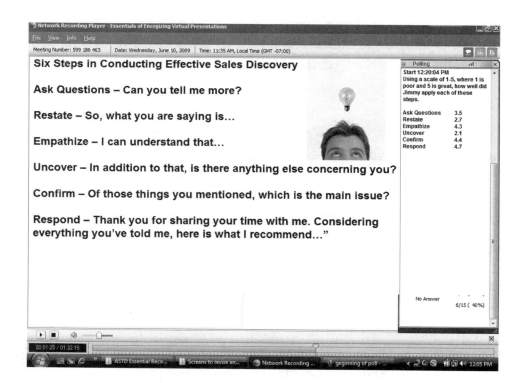

FIGURE 20.1: CONDUCTING EFFECTIVE DISCOVERY

○ Respond—Thank you for sharing that with me. Considering everything you've told me, here is what I recommend . . ."

3. Follow up by playing media presentations of people demonstrating this technique well and demonstrating it poorly. Utilize the chat feature to facilitate a group critique of each demonstration.

4. Continue the presentation by asking participants to demonstrate discovering customer needs and wants effectively, using the microphone feature.

5. Close out this section by conducting a group chat to critique each presentation.

TRY IT YOURSELF

Use Table 20.1 to apply what you covered in this chapter to the presentation that you have been working on since Chapter 16. Review the material in this chapter and clearly identify how you will accomplish several major guidelines in conducting demonstrations.

The Situation

Starion is about to make a major worldwide product introduction. In three months, it will begin taking orders for the Transporter 1000. The

TABLE 20.1 TAKE ACTION FORM: CONDUCTING DEMONSTRATIONS

Major Guideline	How You Will Accomplish It
Make your demonstrations simple.	
Keep your demonstrations "real."	
Make your demonstrations come alive.	

(Continued)

TABLE 20.1 (CONTINUED)

Major Guideline	How You Will Accomplish It
Ensure that your demonstrations are easy to follow.	
Get your audience involved.	

Transporter is the size of a microwave and can digitize and transport a small package from one point to another anywhere in the world, instantly. The Transporter is a completely new product class that has no competition.

The company would like you to conduct a series of virtual presentations to introduce the Transporter 1000 to its 1,000 direct salespeople and its top 3,000 distributors and channel partners. The goal of this effort is to enable personnel to position the benefits and features of the product and demonstrate its compelling usefulness.

As is the case with most revolutionary products, selling the Transporter 1000 will have its challenges. Among them is the price. The price of each unit will be $50,000, and Starion has been unsuccessful in the past in selling equipment at that high a price point.

Starion would like you to lead this effort by collaborating with the sales, marketing, and IT departments. Your management expects you to be the major presenter, but to also include regional sales managers and senior product managers as additional presenters. It expects these virtual presentations to take between 60 and 90 minutes and to utilize portions of presentations that have already been prepared by marketing, as well as several planned collaterals and Web pages.

You have been chosen for this important assignment because of your reputation as a quick learner and a gifted presenter. You are honored, but you are a bit nervous. You are new to conducting virtual presentations, and you have never conducted one of this magnitude.

ASKING AND ANSWERING QUESTIONS

Since the days of Socrates, we as a society have recognized the inherent value of asking questions. As children, most of us asked a million questions a day to gain information about the world. Now, as grown-ups, we still have to rely on questions to gain information, especially during a presentation. You should spend at least 10 percent of your virtual presentation time asking and answering questions. Do not just use questions at the end of your virtual presentation—pepper them throughout the entire event. The only time you should definitely hold questions until the end is when you have a huge audience (and by "huge" I mean triple digits), and that is because if you begin answering questions sooner, you will never be able to move forward.

Many virtual attendees are reticent about asking questions, especially when they know that they can hide. For others, Q&A means that this is the end of the real meat of your presentation, and now is a good time to get going. Sometimes it seems as though the mere mention of the word *questions* has come to be translated as "adios." It's up to you to combat this outcome, though. Questions are a great presentation technique, so don't give up so quickly. This chapter will provide you with a few guidelines for using questions effectively.

The polling feature is one of the best tools in your virtual presentation arsenal, but do not rely exclusively upon polling questions. As with most things in life, you never want to overuse a good thing. Even the most effective strategies become predictable and boring when they are overused.

Many major virtual presentation services and applications incorporate more complex multiple-choice, matching, and fill-in questions. Some even offer grading capabilities, although I'd advise against using them in applications outside of education and training.

The function of most questions and answers is to involve attendees and to give them a chance to pick the presenter's brain. Again, I do not recommend graded questions in applications outside of education and training. It often seems like measuring for the sake of measuring, and it frustrates participants. Now let's take a look at how one might employ a Q&A session in a presentation.

COMPARING VIRTUAL AND FACE-TO-FACE STRATEGIES

Face-to-Face Presentation

Ask questions of individuals or of the group throughout your presentation. If you are asking questions of individuals, when someone answers the question correctly, have him select a participant and ask that participant the next question. Answer attendees' questions at the conclusion of each topic at a minimum. Instead of answering each question yourself, consider throwing the question out to the group to answer. Regardless of who has asked the question, repeat each question and answer for the group, and always recognize attendees for participating.

Virtual Presentation

In a virtual environment, the presenter should ask questions in a manner similar to that used by face-to-face presenters, except that she will use different tools, such as the audio or chat in a virtual presentation. Establish a protocol for participants to ask questions and offer comments. Remind everyone that you will be responding to questions at the conclusion of each topic, using the capabilities of the virtual meeting tool. If you have a moderator, you may encourage participants to submit questions to that person, so that he can merge, cull, and ask you them at the end of each topic.

PRACTICAL HINTS

Here are a few practical hints for asking and answering questions.

Answering Attendees' Questions

- During the planning phase of your presentation, decide how you would like to handle questions from the audience. Would you like attendees to ask questions at any time, ask questions at the conclusion of each topic, or hold questions until the end of your presentation?

- Whenever you answer questions, repeat the question before you answer it. Ask investigative questions that will enable participants to answer the question themselves.

- Do not feel that you have to be the one to answer every question. Take advantage of the knowledge and expertise of the attendees. Redirect the question to the group and then conduct a discussion surrounding the question.

- Finally, when you do not know the answer, admit it and offer to investigate.

Asking Questions

- Ask questions via audio, chat, or writing on the electronic whiteboard.

- Use audio to ask participants questions every now and then with the express purpose of determining whether you are getting your points across clearly or whether more explanation is required.

- Request that participants construct summaries of new information, apply information in real-world scenarios, or answer "what-if" questions.

- Instruct participants to put a symbol (e.g., a raised hand or check mark) by their name when they would like to answer one of your questions.

- It's up to you to manage silence effectively during questioning periods. Give participants time to respond. If you receive no response, make sure that they heard the question. After a reasonable pause, rephrase the question or direct it to a specific participant. If that does not work, you can always have your producer/moderator use a prepared answer to get the ball rolling.

REAL-WORLD EXAMPLE

The following is an example from a virtual presentation exploring the duties of a customer service agent. The steps identify the actions of the presenter of this virtual presentation in asking and answering questions.

I. Ask the following polling questions.

    A. Which of the following options is our top priority, resolving customer difficulties or selling additional products?

    B. Who feels that he is in a customer service position and who feels that he is in a sales position? Pick one or the other, even if neither fits quite right (see Figure 21.1).

    C. What percentage of your compensation is based upon sales volume?

II. Display the results of the polling during the activity or afterward. Then drive the point home by asking attendees to write on the

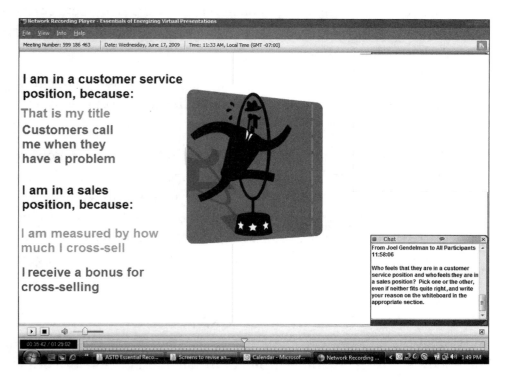

FIGURE 21.1: ROLE OF A SERVICE AGENT

electronic whiteboard what they feel are the main points of the discussion.

TRY IT YOURSELF

Use Table 21.1 to apply what you covered in this chapter to the presentation that you have been working on since Chapter 16.

The Situation

Starion is about to make a major worldwide product introduction. In three months, it will begin taking orders for the Transporter 1000. The Transporter is the size of a microwave and can digitize and transport a small package from one point to another anywhere in the world, instantly. The Transporter is a completely new product class that has no competition.

The company would like you to conduct a series of virtual presentations to introduce the Transporter 1000 to its 1,000 direct salespeople and its top 3,000 distributors and channel partners. The goal of this effort is to enable personnel to position the benefits and features of the product and demonstrate its compelling usefulness.

As is the case with most revolutionary products, selling the Transporter 1000 will have its challenges. Among them is the price. The price of each unit will be $50,000, and Starion has been unsuccessful in the past in selling equipment at that high a price point.

Starion would like you to lead this effort by collaborating with the sales, marketing, and IT departments. Your management expects you to be the major presenter, but to also include regional sales managers and senior product managers as additional presenters. It expects these virtual presentations to take between 60 and 90 minutes and to utilize portions of presentations that have already been prepared by marketing, as well as several planned collaterals and Web pages.

You have been chosen for this important assignment because of your reputation as a quick learner and a gifted presenter. You are honored, but

TABLE 21.1 TAKE ACTION FORM: ASKING AND ANSWERING QUESTIONS

Questions	Expected or Planned Answers
Questions that you intend to ask:	
Questions that you expect to be asked:	

you are a bit nervous. You are new to conducting virtual presentations, and you have never conducted one of this magnitude.

Take a moment now to identify the four most important questions that you intend to ask and the four most prevalent questions that you expect members of the audience to ask you. Additionally, identify the answers that you expect or that you intend to use. Utilize Table 21.1.

INITIATING AND MANAGING DISCUSSIONS

Discussions are a great way to create a shared experience during your presentation by getting audience members truly involved. Most experienced presenters know that discussions look deceptively easy. In truth, they are anything but. Since you are not physically present in a virtual presentation, you lack the element of control that someone who is there in person has in reining in a discussion. This is not an insurmountable problem, though; your relative distance in the virtual world just means that you need to hold the reins a bit tighter. That means clearly identifying the purpose and output of the discussion, monitoring discussion chats closely, making comments that summarize individual postings, and redirecting the discussion back to the topic if necessary.

COMPARING VIRTUAL AND FACE-TO-FACE STRATEGIES

Face-to-Face Presentation

In a face-to-face presentation, one solid method for introducing a discussion is by displaying a newspaper headline or sharing a quote that pertains to the topic. Then you can summarize on a flipchart the issues that your quote or headline stirs up and break the audience into separate groups so that they can address each issue. Assign three of your most astute attendees to be judges. While the groups are preparing, roam the room to make sure that each group is on target.

Ask a representative of each group to present that group's conclusions to the larger group. As each group presents, interrupt and ask more probing questions. Since successful presentations need to be brief, provide each group with only a limited amount of time to present. Direct the discussion verbally, and add support by making notes on the flipchart. At the conclusion of all the presentations, ask the judges you selected to identify the strengths of each presentation and determine which group was the most convincing. Provide the winning group with a symbolic prize, such as a paperweight, backpack, or pen and pencil set incorporating your company's logo, and thank all attendees for their openness and participation.

Virtual Presentation

The same method for starting a discussion can easily be duplicated in a virtual format. One of the main differences between the face-to-face and virtual strategies is that you do not need to separate the attendees into groups, since virtual meeting tools provide you with the capabilities to manage larger numbers of participants effectively. As a presenter, you would still introduce a provoking topic by displaying a headline or a quote. Summarize the main issues that are raised on your electronic whiteboard. Ask participants to address each issue by speaking or sending you their thoughts via chat. While they are getting their observations across, you should continue to ask more probing questions, using the chat function. If the discussion lags, ask your producer/moderator to get things going, using prearranged questions or comments. Such questions, and your responses to them, will help direct the discussion, and you can emphasize these points by making notes on the whiteboard. If you wish to measure where attendees stand on the issue you're discussing, conduct a poll and display the results. Bring the threads of the discussion together by reiterating the points on the whiteboard, which should lead you to some conclusion. Send a private thank-you e-mail to the attendees who were most involved in the discussion, and verbally thank all participants for their openness and participation.

SEVEN STRATEGIES FOR CONDUCTING EFFECTIVE DISCUSSIONS

Here are seven strategies for initiating and managing discussions. Each of these strategies is discussed in some great detail. Together, they form the foundation for any discussion in either a face-to-face or a virtual presentation.

1. Initiate the Discussion

Ask a thought-provoking or timely question, such as, "Can your firm succeed by simply doing more with less, or are you compelled to do things differently and better?" Voice or express a potentially unreasonable opinion (e.g., "Why do you need to change the way you have always done things? Didn't everything work out well before?"). Display a poignant cartoon or a thoughtful quote. We have included many such quotes in this book. Continue by identifying the specific outcomes you expect from the discussion. Give participants roles during discussions. Some of these roles are

- Facilitator to initiate a discussion with one or two questions from the content.

- Process observer to monitor the presentation dynamics, ensure that everyone is involved in discussions and participates, bring conversations back on track, and offer a brief report at the end.

- Summarizer to outline the main topics discussed, the points that participants made, and the conclusions reached by the group.

2. Structure the Discussion

No other activity can get as far out of control as quickly as a discussion. For example, attendees can speak over each other, participants may become argumentative, and the discussion itself can go off on an unproductive tangent. Be sure to display or distribute an outline of the discussion, and enforce it.

- Clarify the theme of the discussion and the topics that you expect it to cover.

- Begin with a vague question and ask the audience members to further refine the question, answer it, and then identify why they made the choices that they did. This provides the group with some higher-level activities, such as making additions to the structure of the presentation.

- Separate a discussion into separate questions and assign each question to one of several groups. You may assign each group to a different breakout room. At the conclusion, conduct a group discussion that ties together the various groups' contributions.

3. Control the Flow of Discussion

This step requires "ruling with an iron hand in a velvet glove." The more controversial the discussion, the more you will need to control it and keep it focused on the subject. Be ready to step in quickly to redirect the discussion toward the goal. Throughout all of this, attempt to maintain a positive and helpful tone and demeanor.

- Closely manage the discussion by asking another colleague to help you monitor the activity from a content standpoint. Ask your producer/moderator to take care of the technical details.

- Use the microphone, whiteboard, chat window, or e-mail to keep the discussion on track by:

  - Commenting on the group's progress (e.g., whether the group's comments seem clear and relevant).

  - Dealing with disruptive participants quickly and kindly, using private chat postings or e-mails to help them see how they are coming across to others.

  - Resolving differences of opinion by encouraging participants to explore and identify outside resources (e.g., reference materials in folders or links to Web sites).

4. Provoke Respectful Controversy

Respectful controversy occurs when people may strongly disagree in a discussion, but they never take it personally and certainly don't insult each other. This rule is certainly a double-edged sword. In one sense, you want to encourage participants to express their beliefs and values and passionately link the discussion to their life and work. One the other hand, you need to always model, manage, and reinforce participants' respectful behavior toward their colleagues.

5. Help Participants Listen to One Another

All of us are guilty of hearing only what we want to hear. Summarize each comment. Review and draw together the threads of the discussion. Clarify comments and ask questions to ensure that each voice is not only heard, but understood.

- Plant ideas by asking a leading question on the electronic whiteboard or displaying it in the chat window. A leading question could be, "Do you agree with this?" "How would you handle this?" "Have you ever seen anyone do this really well?" "How did they do it?" or "What would you do in their shoes?"

- Provide summaries that explicitly reference participants' comments.

- Encourage diverse viewpoints. Tap participants' unique knowledge or perspective. Use e-mail or private chat postings to request comments from selected individuals who you feel can provide a unique perspective.

- Draw out participants who seem to be missing the discussion by initially using a private chat posting or e-mail to ensure that they are not having technology or skill problems. Then indicate how useful their perspective is to the discussion and how much you would value their contribution.

6. Bring Together Diverse Threads into a Summary

Surely you want to draw together the discussion at the end, but consider including mini-reviews throughout longer and meatier discussions.

- Weave together attendees' comments and connect participants' contributions to the theme of the discussion.

- Always end by restating the goals of the discussion, summarizing the results, and relating the results to the next topic.

7. Thank All Participants for Their Contributions

Some participants may feel that they went out on a limb to express an unpopular opinion. Thank them for being courageous and highlight that this would be a boring world without different opinions. You may also add a personal chat to those attendees who you feel contributed significantly to the discussion.

REAL-WORLD EXAMPLE

The following is an example from a virtual presentation exploring the duties of a customer service agent. The steps identify the actions of the presenter of this virtual presentation in conducting a discussion.

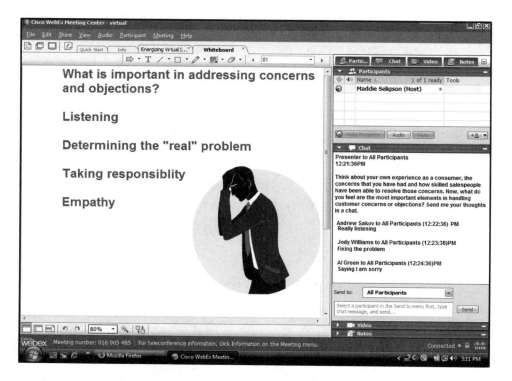

FIGURE 22.1: IMPORTANT ELEMENTS IN RESPONDING TO CONCERNS AND OBJECTIONS

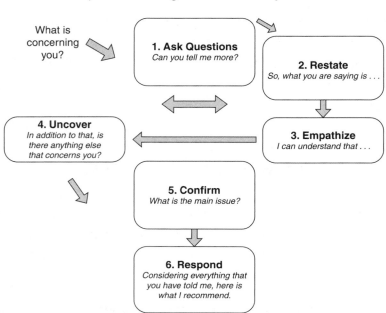

Steps for Handling Concerns or Objections

FIGURE 22.2: STEPS IN HANDLING CONCERNS OR OBJECTIONS (A)

1. Use the chat feature and whiteboard discussion to identify the important elements of responding to concerns or objections (see Figure 22.1).

2. Then display a graphic of the process (see Figures 22.2 and 22.3) and use the chat feature to discuss how the model incorporates the important elements that are listed on the whiteboard and in this process.

TRY IT YOURSELF

Use Table 22.1 to apply what you covered in this chapter to the presentation that you have been working on since Chapter 16. Review the material in this chapter and clearly identify how you will accomplish several major guidelines in initiating and managing discussions.

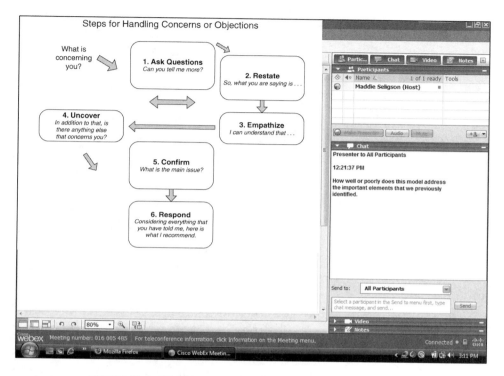

FIGURE 22.3: STEPS IN HANDLING CONCERNS OR OBJECTIONS (B)

The Situation

Starion is about to make a major worldwide product introduction. In three months, it will begin taking orders for the Transporter 1000. The

TABLE 22.1 TAKE ACTION FORM: INITIATING AND MANAGING DISCUSSIONS

Major Guideline	How You Will Accomplish It
Setting up or provoking the discussion	
Managing the discussion	
Keeping the discussion moving	

TABLE 22.1 (CONTINUED)

Major Guideline	How You Will Accomplish It
Summarizing the discussion	
Promoting interaction	

Transporter is the size of a microwave and can digitize and transport a small package from one point to another anywhere in the world, instantly. The Transporter is a completely new product class that has no competition.

The company would like you to conduct a series of virtual presentations to introduce the Transporter 1000 to its 1,000 direct salespeople and its top 3,000 distributors and channel partners. The goal of this effort is to enable personnel to position the benefits and features of the product and demonstrate its compelling usefulness.

As is the case with most revolutionary products, selling the Transporter 1000 will have its challenges. Among them is the price. The price of each unit will be $50,000, and Starion has been unsuccessful in the past in selling equipment at that high a price point.

Starion would like you to lead this effort by collaborating with the sales, marketing, and IT departments. Your management expects you to be the major presenter, but also to include regional sales managers and senior product managers as additional presenters. It expects these virtual presentations to take between 60 and 90 minutes and to utilize portions of presentations that have already been prepared by marketing, as well as several planned collaterals and Web pages.

You have been chosen for this important assignment because of your reputation as a quick learner and a gifted presenter. You are honored, but you are a bit nervous. You are new to conducting virtual presentations, and you have never conducted one of this magnitude.

23

PROMOTING INTERACTION

Throughout this book, we have discussed the importance of encouraging interaction in your virtual presentations. This chapter is dedicated to guiding you in enhancing your interaction with attendees and the interaction between attendees. Interaction is critical to any presentation. We are social animals, and we typically enjoy working with others. These interactions also encourage doing. Both *interacting* and *doing* provide your attendees with opportunities to internalize the information in your virtual presentation and make it their own.

Interacting is easy when the other parties are in the same room; it's a bit more difficult when they are not. But we successfully interact virtually with people all the time. We send e-mails, write notes, talk on the telephone, text message, and some of us even Skype. So in promoting interaction in virtual meetings, we are only enhancing skills that we rely on every day.

INTERACTIONS WILL MAKE YOUR VIRTUAL PRESENTATIONS MORE DYNAMIC

Very few speakers are so polished and compelling that people will stand up clapping or wave their arms in the air. To consistently affect people in that way, you would need to be a politician, a religious leader, or Tony Robbins. Most of us need to earn that type of intensity, and we do so by creating meaningful interactions with our audience. As we all know, dynamic interactions do not just happen. We plan them, fine-tune them, and practice them until they are predictably fantastic.

POLLING IS A GOOD FIRST STEP

Enticing attendees to participate in your virtual meeting by including polls or typed questions and responses is a step in the right direction, but remember to frame these questions in terms of their value to the audience, not to you. If you start your presentation with a poll asking people to provide you with sales-oriented information, you put them on the defensive. Make sure that you have *given value* to your listeners before you *demand value* from them. Each time you ask for information, tell them how answering your question will benefit them: "This step will help me customize our session to make sure that I address the things that you want to hear about." If you receive typed comments or questions from the audience, refer to the questioner by first name, putting a personal touch on the communication and letting attendees know that you are truly paying attention to them as individuals.

The Truth about Polling

Do not expect 100 percent participation in the polls. Give participants adequate time to respond, but do not slow down the action. It is a bit like waiting for a bag of popcorn to pop. First you hear bursts of popping, and then it just trickles down to a gradual halt. Close the poll when the responding trickles down. You also do not want to give participants a chance to change their answers when they see that they have given an unpopular one. Some seasoned virtual presenters keep the results of the poll hidden until the end of the poll. It's boring when everyone agrees.

IMAGINE IT AND YOU WILL BE THERE

When you are planning your virtual presentation:

1. Close your eyes and imagine that your audience is in front of you. What would you do if you were face-to-face with an audience? Keep this in your mind's eye until you can feel the activity and experience its energy.

2. Now imagine what you would do if you and the audience could not see you or each other. How would you use your voice, your words, canned demonstrations, or outside materials to achieve the same effect? Gather your imagination until you can feel yourself in the middle of it. You are observing the attendees and reacting to them. Then ride it out in your mind. See how it goes. Fine-tune it and play it out.

3. Once you have done and completed all this, write it down.

Good interactions also need to be rehearsed and fine-tuned. So before the big day, rehearse interactive activities with friends and colleagues just as you would presentations and demonstrations, and smooth out any rough spots.

USE PLANTED QUESTIONS

OK, this may sound a bit shady, but as William Shakespeare wrote in *As you Like It*, "All the world's a stage, and all the men and women merely players." Sometimes you just need to prime the pump to get things started. If the presentation is quiet or if you ask if anyone has a question and no one answers, have your producer/moderator ask one that you have prepared in advance. He can ask you the question via audio or chat. You may also want it to appear that your attendees are running the show, when they are really only following your script. If you want to be tricky, use the chat feature to secretly request that selected attendees ask such planted questions. You can even make up a question and attribute it to some mythical attendee. Say, "Emily from San Francisco would like to know. . ." Forget that there is no Emily. No one is watching the chat as closely as you and your producer/moderator are. You may feel that this is a bit deceptive, and it is. If you don't feel comfortable with this technique, feel free not to include it in your arsenal of tricks.

THREE ARE BETTER THAN TWO

If you are planning any types of activities in your virtual presentations that involve pairs of attendees, such as case studies or team contests, try using three attendees instead of two. For example, if you place pairs of attendees in breakout rooms where one plays the role of the salesperson and other plays the role of a customer, consider throwing in a third to play a sales manager with the job of rating the performance of the other two. Since having three players can be confusing, I recommend that you summarize the instructions for interactive activities on the electronic whiteboard.

TRY IT YOURSELF

Use Table 23.1 to apply what you covered in this chapter to the presentation that you have been working on since Chapter 16. Review the material

TABLE 23.1 TAKE ACTION FORM: PROMOTING INTERACTION

Idea 1
Idea 2

and then identify two ideas that you have for promoting interaction during the presentation.

The Situation

Starion is about to make a major worldwide product introduction. In three months, it will begin taking orders for the Transporter 1000. The Transporter is the size of a microwave and can digitize and transport a small package from one point to another anywhere in the world, instantly. The Transporter is a completely new product class that has no competition.

The company would like you to conduct a series of virtual presentations to introduce the Transporter 1000 to its 1,000 direct salespeople and its top 3,000 distributors and channel partners. The goal of this effort is to enable personnel to position the benefits and features of the product and demonstrate its compelling usefulness.

As is the case with most revolutionary products, selling the Transporter 1000 will have its challenges. Among them is the price. The price of each unit will be $50,000, and Starion has been unsuccessful in the past in selling equipment at that high a price point.

Starion would like you to lead this effort by collaborating with the sales, marketing, and IT departments. Your management expects you to be the major presenter, but to also include regional sales managers and senior product managers as additional presenters. It expects these virtual presentations to take between 60 and 90 minutes and to utilize portions of presentations that have already been prepared by marketing, as well as several planned collaterals and Web pages.

You have been chosen for this important assignment because of your reputation as a quick learner and a gifted presenter. You are honored, but you are a bit nervous. You are new to conducting virtual presentations, and you have never conducted one of this magnitude.

24

UTILIZING ASSESSMENTS AND EVALUATIONS

Virtual presentations have the capabilities for your conducing assessments and evaluations by using polling questions. Typically these are limited to yes/no, true/false, and multiple-choice questions. You may ask a true/false or multiple-choice question and see how many participants selected each response. These types of assessment activities may be used to wake up participants, determine their level of engagement in the presentation, identify where participants stand on particular issues, or evaluate their competence.

COMPARING VIRTUAL AND FACE-TO-FACE STRATEGIES

Face-to-Face Presentation

In face-to-face presentations, good presenters assess and evaluate participants' performance using group question-and-answer sessions, individual and group quizzes, and formal assessments.

Virtual Presentation

The strongest tool that virtual presentations have for conducting assessments is the polling feature. You can keep these results to yourself or share them with all participants. If you wish, you can also pose a question on the electronic whiteboard and ask attendees to write their answers, each using a different color marker. This is sometimes a bit more fun and involving for your participants.

PRACTICAL HINTS

Here are some guidelines, hints, and ideas that you may find helpful in utilizing assessments and evaluations.

- **When to use assessments.** Use knowledge checks frequently during the presentation to confirm your participants' understanding (at the end of each section at a minimum). This could just be a couple of spontaneous questions sprinkled throughout your presentation—there doesn't have to be a formal assessment activity.

- **How to use them efficiently.** Here's how to get the most mileage out of your assessments:

  ○ Include enough time in your presentation schedule for spontaneous assessments.

- Ask questions that are clear, pertinent, brief, and challenging.

- Provide feedback that is timely, relevant, and specific. Avoid feedback that is brief or abrupt. Attendees may interpret such feedback as angry, which is an unwanted impression that is hard to come back from.

- **Format and types of questions.** Utilize true/false, yes/no, or multiple-choice questions. Include questions that match the information that you are presenting and the degree of knowledge of the attendees. In addition to using questions that ask attendees to regurgitate facts and figures, use some that require them to use the information incorporated in your virtual presentation by evaluating proposed solutions and applying the information you provided to new situations.

- **Try something new.** Use fun assessment activities, such as games and simulations. These may include hangman, crossword puzzles, and word searches to test anything from new terminology to the benefits associated with the features of a new product. Alternatively, ask attendees to type on the electronic whiteboard as many words as come to mind about a topic covered in your virtual presentation. Encourage participants to enter as many words as they can think of in three minutes, no editing required. Review the responses with the entire group. In the interests of time, keep your games short and simple.

- **Video assessments.** Because most people are visual learners, you might want to consider playing a multimedia demonstration of a good example and a poor example of the subject of your presentation. You may then conduct a poll to assess whether the audience can tell which is which and explain why.

- **Are we done yet?** One very skilled virtual presenter uses an attention meter as part of his presentation. At any time during his virtual presentation, attendees can identify how interested they are in the topic and how much they would like to move on. This information is summarized as the length of a bar, similar to the bar that identifies how much battery life you have left in your PDA, cell phone, or camera. The presenter then uses this meter to determine when to continue the discussion of a topic and when to move on.

HOW TO MAKE USING ASSESSMENTS AND EVALUATIONS EASIER FOR YOU

- Have groups use materials and assessment instruments (e.g., lists of questions) that are located in a shared folder to complete in-basket activities. For example, if the presentation were on reviewing employee performance, you might ask the groups to determine the strengths and weaknesses of an employee and create a professional development plan using a blank plan and referring to a sample plan, both located in a shared folder.

- Remember, your job is not to be the sage on the stage, but to be the guide on the side. Do not feel the need to interpret the results of a poll. Have your moderator do it. Better yet, draw upon the expertise of the group by asking one of the attendees how she would interpret the results or asking the group for an interpretation by initiating a chat.

- When you are conducting a poll, do not rush. Give people a little time to think—about 30 seconds, and no more. Definitely ask them to raise their hand symbol when they are done so that you can determine when everyone is finished.

- You do not need to respond to every attendee answer or comment. Limiting your responses is extremely useful if you are presenting to a large audience. When you ask a question, request that attendees respond using the chat tool. Do not react to all answers, but choose just a few. Ask your producer/moderator to pick a number from 1 to 5, and respond to answers corresponding to that number. For example, if the producer/moderator picks the numbers 3 and 5, provide feedback on the third and fifth answers.

- Use additional question-and-answer tools, such as Adobe Breeze Presenter, for more robust assessments and evaluations.

REAL-WORLD EXAMPLE

If you are delivering a presentation to telesales personnel on using transition statements to move from discovery to closing, you may assess or evaluate participants' skills by asking them to demonstrate this technique using audio. You may then use the polling feature to conduct a group assessment, using questions similar to the following:

1. Was the transition statement used at the appropriate time: turning the corner from discovery to closing?

2. Rate the strength of the transition statement.

3. Did you feel that the speaker earned the right to move from discovery to closing?

4. Did the transition seem sincere?

You can then use another set of questions to summarize the activity and provoke some reflection. This set may include

1. Generally, how well did attendees do in using transition statements?

2. Which transition statement was the strongest and why?

3. Which statement sounded the most sincere?

4. Which transition statements would apply to your selling environment?

TRY IT YOURSELF

Use Table 24.1 to apply what you covered in this chapter to the presentation that you have been working on since Chapter 16. Review the material in this chapter and clearly identify some new and different types of assessments you intend to use, how you could use assessments to overcome silence, and what you plan to do to make conducting assessments easier for you.

The Situation

Starion is about to make a major worldwide product introduction. In three months, it will begin taking orders for the Transporter 1000. The Transporter is the size of a microwave and can digitize and transport a small

TABLE 24.1 TAKE ACTION FORM: UTILIZING ASSESSMENTS AND EVALUATIONS

Major Guideline	How You Will Accomplish It
Some new and different ideas	
Overcoming silence	
Making it easier for you	

package from one point to another anywhere in the world, instantly. The Transporter is a completely new product class that has no competition.

The company would like you to conduct a series of virtual presentations to introduce the Transporter 1000 to its 1,000 direct salespeople and its top 3,000 distributors and channel partners. The goal of this effort is to enable personnel to position the benefits and features of the product and demonstrate its compelling usefulness.

As is the case with most revolutionary products, selling the Transporter 1000 will have its challenges. Among them is the price. The price of each unit will be $50,000, and Starion has been unsuccessful in the past in selling equipment at that high a price point.

Starion would like you to lead this effort by collaborating with the sales, marketing, and IT departments. Your management expects you to be the major presenter, but to also include regional sales managers and senior product managers as additional presenters. It expects these virtual presentations to take between 60 and 90 minutes and to utilize portions of presentations that have already been prepared by marketing, as well as several planned collaterals and Web pages.

You have been chosen for this important assignment because of your reputation as a quick learner and a gifted presenter. You are honored, but you are a bit nervous. You are new to conducting virtual presentations, and you have never conducted one of this magnitude.

STRATEGIES FOR CREATING EXCITEMENT AND MOTIVATION

Despite what some presenters seem to think, you can never bore someone into embracing you ideas or purchasing your product. Virtual presentations do not have to be sterile and uninspiring. On the contrary, they can be dynamic and memorable, but it all depends on what the presenter brings to the table. Creating and sustaining motivation and excitement is probably the greatest challenge in a face-to-face, virtual, or any other kind of presentation. Think of the best presentations that you have had the pleasure of being involved in. What did the presenters do to create such enthusiasm? Were you the only one who was excited, or did the other audience members seem to feel the same way?

Here are some major strategies for creating excitement and motivation in your presentations.

EIGHT STRATEGIES FOR GETTING PEOPLE FIRED UP

1. **Know your audience.** Determine the relevant characteristics of participants and the presentation setting by:

   ○ Sending e-mails to participants prior to the presentation to determine what makes them tick. (For example, what excites them about their job? What do they enjoy doing outside of work?) There may be some situations in which this action may not be appropriate, particularly if the attendees do not know much about you or your company. In that case, you can gather information on the group as a whole by researching industry or professional groups. You may also wish to Google particular attendees or review their profile on social networking sites, such as LinkedIn or Facebook. You will be surprised at what you can find. Just as a caution, keep whatever information you do find to yourself. Most people don't feel comfortable being snooped on.

   ○ Polling attendees at the beginning of the presentation to determine similar information.

2. **Use a wide variety of presentation activities and media.** Build suspense by creating activities whose results are not predictable, such as flexible role playing. Feel free to change the rules while the activities are still in motion, perhaps altering the prospect's real budget or buying criteria. You may do this using either the whiteboard or the chat tool. Once you have separated attendees into groups and breakout rooms, you can also use selective chats and different shared folders to provide different groups with separate rules and instructions.

3. **Foster collaboration.** Facilitate collaborative group activities, such as brainstorming exercises. As we discussed earlier, separate the attendees into groups and assign each group to its own breakout area. Be sure to assign a leader for each group. Store the materials for each group in a separate shared folder to provide groups with unique instructions.

4. **Build relationships.** Arrive early for your session and chat with attendees. Ask participants to share something about themselves, why they are there, and how they anticipate using the information that they will glean from the presentation. Also encourage attendees to chat with each other. If your presentation is long enough to include lunch, plan virtual lunches, where people can communicate while nibbling on a sandwich at their desks. If your presentation contains multiple sessions, be sure to stay in contact between sessions.

5. **Use discovery techniques.** Use discovery techniques to guide attendees in acquiring information. It is very much like leading them down the garden path and having them pick their own fruit. Using discovery techniques, such as Knowledge Easter Egg Hunts using attendees' resources (e.g., Web sites), they discover information on their own.

6. **Be prepared for anything.** Anticipate participants' questions and difficulties, and prepare standard answers and remedial material in advance. When presenting salespeople with information on a new product, prepare answers to questions such as, what makes this product so great? How is it different from our current product? What will be our competition? How are we better? What are the main features of this new project? How will they benefit potential customers? Being prepared for anything will make conducting discussions and questioning sessions easier—it's something that you can pull out of your bag of tricks just when you need it.

7. **Establish and maintain an exciting environment.**

○ Create a self-running presentation that attendees can view as they enter the virtual session but before the presentation begins. Include presenter and participant bios, photos, and an exciting agenda using catchy-sounding topic titles (e.g., "Presenting Benefits of the DXT 6000 That Will Rock Your Clients' World"). You can even arrange a pre-presentation trailer.

○ Listen actively to attendee chats. Resist the temptation to judge their comments.

○ Notice patterns in chats and posting. Make comments that recognize, summarize, and weave together discussion threads.

○ Be attentive when participants are not being authentic or genuine, but instead are telling you what they feel you want them to say or what is the "right" answer.

  ○ Carefully review postings.

  ○ Respond honestly.

  ○ Call or send a private posting or e-mail assuring them that their comments to you are confidential and that you are keenly interested in their honest opinion.

○ Create constructive conflict or "creative abrasion" by

  ○ Asking leading questions, such as, "What clients are interested in making more capital expenditures in this challenging financial environment?"

  ○ Representing points of view that differ from the company party line.

  ○ Exploring the content in a new context. For example, in George Orwell's *Animal Farm*, the author used the metaphor of a farm to illustrate the dangers of the leaders of a revolution turning into copies of those they ousted. I know of a company that presented basic and advanced financial concepts in the context of a lemonade stand. Using this simplified and comfortable example made understanding complex financial concepts easy and made the company a ton of money.

8. **Use interactive and attendee-delivered lectures.** Try interactive lectures where you plant and distribute questions to both the producer/moderator and the attendees. One example of an interactive lecture is to place a number on each question. At various junctures in your presentation, simply ask for the next question. See Chapter 23 for more information.

REAL-WORLD EXAMPLE

Ask selected participants to describe a personal customer service issue where they were the customer and they became irate. Then use the polling feature to determine how members of the group would have handled the call, using an effective discovery technique. Here are some questions that you might use:

1. Did the listener ask appropriate questions?

2. Did the listener confirm and emphasize his understanding?

3. Did the listener correctly diagnose and solve the problem?

4. Did the agent meet the emotional needs of the speaker?

Finally, ask the previously "irate" participant if this technique would have worked in her situation. Repeat this strategy for one or two additional attendees.

TRY IT YOURSELF

Use Table 25.1 to apply what you covered in this chapter to the presentation that you have been working on since Chapter 16. Review the material in this chapter and clearly identify how you will achieve several major guidelines for creating excitement and motivation.

The Situation

Starion is about to make a major worldwide product introduction. In three months, it will begin taking orders for the Transporter 1000. The Transporter is the size of a microwave and can digitize and transport a small package from one point to another anywhere in the world, instantly. The Transporter is a completely new product class that has no competition.

TABLE 25.1 TAKE ACTION FORM: CREATING EXCITEMENT AND MOTIVATION

Major Guideline	How You Will Accomplish It
Knowing your audience	
Fostering collaboration	
Employing discovery techniques	
Effectively using discussions and questioning	
Establishing and maintaining a warm and exciting environment	

The company would like you to conduct a series of virtual presentations to introduce the Transporter 1000 to its 1,000 direct salespeople and its top 3,000 distributors and channel partners. The goal of this effort is to enable personnel to position the benefits and features of the product and demonstrate its compelling usefulness.

As is the case with most revolutionary products, selling the Transporter 1000 will have its challenges. Among them is the price. The price of each unit will be $50,000, and Starion has been unsuccessful in the past in selling equipment at that high a price point.

Starion would like you to lead this effort by collaborating with the sales, marketing, and IT departments. Your management expects you to be the major presenter, but to also include regional sales managers and senior product managers as additional presenters. It expects these virtual presentations to take between 60 and 90 minutes and to utilize portions of presentations that have already been prepared by marketing, as well as several planned collaterals and Web pages.

You have been chosen for this important assignment because of your reputation as a quick learner and a gifted presenter. You are honored, but you are a bit nervous. You are new to conducting virtual presentations, and you have never conducted one of this magnitude.

FACILITATING VIRTUAL PRESENTATIONS FOR TEAMS

Most of the employees in the workforce today belong to several geographically dispersed work teams. You may be in the same department or simply be assigned to the same project. Your team may be composed of employees from the same company plus some outside resources. Some teams are made up of personnel from many different companies. The one commonality is that you all need to work together to get the job done. That being the case, there is a good chance that one day you will be asked to conduct a virtual presentation that involves teams. It can be difficult to get everyone on a team to work together well, but I do have some thoughts on conducting virtual presentations with teams:

- **If they work together as teams, you may as well present to them as teams.** Most virtual presentation applications and services provide you with the capability to establish separate breakout rooms. If you are working with several different teams, you may assign each team to a separate breakout room for discussions and small group activities, such as what concerns or requirements they might have in selecting a new product or service.

- **Always be watching.** If you have sufficient resources, assign a moderator to act as a facilitator for each team. If not, appoint a member of each team as a facilitator and be sure to provide him with detailed instructions, just as you would for any table group activity in a face-to-face presentation. Roam around the room virtually by poking your head into each breakout room to see how groups are doing and to help teams stay on track if they misunderstood the instructions or have gone off on a tangent.

- **Always reintegrate the group.** Even though you dispersed the group into teams in their own breakout rooms, you still want to continue the presentation as a cohesive group. A good method for doing that is to return participants to the larger group at the conclusion of the presentation and ask each team to conduct a short recap.

- **Walk the talk.** Regardless of the topic of your presentation, when you are conducting a presentation for teams, you want to make sure that you exemplify the team's values, processes, and behaviors. You can accomplish this by interviewing attendees or their managers in advance of your session, reviewing any associated documents, and incorporating those values and processes into your presentation.

ENDING WITH A BANG

The ending of your presentation should be its pinnacle, not its abyss. Everything that you have done so far should lead up to this crescendo. I recommend that you never end a presentation with a dry restatement of the agenda. Never say, "Let's summarize what we've learned today." Go back to why attendees are there in the first place. If the presentation was meant to address a problem or a yearning, do not simply remind them of that fact. Get them to feel it.

Creating a feeling rather than describing it is one of the most basic differences between standard writing and poetry. Standard communication tells you that it is snowing, but poetry compels you to feel the coldness and wetness of the snow. It evokes the emotion of what it was like when you were a child, saw the pure white blanket, and felt that thrilling sense of not having to go to school. Go back to your introduction, conjure up the hopes and dreams that participants had at the beginning of the presentation, and help them imagine what it will feel like when they realize those dreams.

Focus on enabling attendees to answer the following questions:

- Why did they come here? What was their goal?

- What will they do tomorrow, in a week, and in a month to attain that goal?

- What was their experience like?

- What type of support can they expect from you, or from others?

- What will success be like for them personally?

- How will you continue what you have started today?

COMPARING VIRTUAL AND FACE-TO-FACE STRATEGIES

Face-to-Face Presentation

Reestablish the relevance of your presentation by flashing headlines, stories, or statistics similar to the ones that you used in the section of your presentation in which you established relevance. Ask participants how they felt at the beginning of the presentation and how they feel now. Conduct a short discussion on what they might do differently as a result of this presentation. Ask attendees to complete a short feedback form and pass it to the front of the rooms. Present a short media presentation of "happy endings," or success stories in which interviewees offer testimonials on how they handled such situations in the past, how they handled one after one of your presentations, and the difference that it made. Present your contact information for future questions. Thank the participants for their time and involvement, and offer to remain after the presentation to answer questions.

Virtual Presentation

Use a strategy similar to the one that you used to establish relevance, except with even more persuasive stories, articles, and statistics. Utilize the polling feature or conduct a chat to determine how attendees felt before the presentation and how they feel now. Ask them to ponder the situation that brought them here, how they could have addressed it differently, and the results they could have enjoyed. Ask your producer/moderator to select the most compelling responses and summarize them for the group. Ask participants to take no more than 60 seconds to complete an online feedback form, and be sure to include the URL that they may use to access it. If attendees need more than 60 seconds to complete a feedback form, they are overthinking it. Personalize the ending by using the electronic whiteboard to summarize a "before and after" story of your own.

Finally, the producer/moderator will ask a couple of planted questions regarding how attendees can get in touch with you after the presentation. Don't just answer via audio—display. Send contact information to participants, and offer them a few "office hours" when you will be online and available to answer questions or to discuss related issues further. Thank participants for their time and involvement. Ask attendees to log off or stay in the meeting if they have brief questions that they would like to have answered. Ensure that all attendees are logged off the meeting before discussing the presentation with the other presenters, or begin a separate meeting or telephone call, just to be safe.

PRACTICAL HINTS

Here are some guidelines, hints, and ideas that you may find helpful in ending with a bang.

Two Great Unfounded Fears

Most presenters have two unfounded fears: (1) that they will finish their presentation early, and (2) that they will not have enough time to share all the information that they wanted to cover. Since most of us are well versed in the subject matter of our virtual presentation, we feel that we have a great deal of knowledge to share and would like to share as much of it as we can with our attendees. Often, we overestimate the amount of knowledge that suits our goals and attendees' patience. Whenever possible, slim down your virtual presentation so that you can end on time. Most of us have complained when presentations ran over, but I do not think that anybody has ever complained when one ended early. We are typically overjoyed that we have a few moments in which to send an e-mail or make a call before our next meeting. Finally, it is far better to leave your audience hungry for more than overwhelmed or bored with having received too much. Let the attendees crave a bit more, so that they will explore on their own, attend your more advanced presentation, or look forward to a follow-up call.

Receiving Feedback

One of the best ways to improve your methodology is to solicit some feedback on how well your presentation went. As I've mentioned before, there are several ways to do this, such as asking attendees to complete a feedback form or a survey. You may also feel that if they do not complete the form while they are in the presentation, they never will. You are probably right! My recommendation is that you think very hard about what type of feedback you really need and keep your questions to a bare minimum. Reasonable requests are:

- How likely are you to use the skills covered in this presentation within the next week?

- Are you interested in knowing more about how our event management services can make planning your next event more convenient?

- How comfortable do you feel with your knowledge of our new medical plan? Are there any areas that you still find unclear?

- Would you like to stay in touch? How (e-mail or phone) and when?

Be very specific, and do not ask for information that you are not sure you will use. Regardless of how much time you give them, participants will probably spend less than a minute providing you with information, so choose what you request wisely. You can always send a more detailed questionnaire in a day or two.

Table 27.1 contains an example of a simple feedback form.

TABLE 27.1 FEEDBACK FORM

Thank you for attending!

Please use this form to identify how well this presentation met your needs and how we may be able to contact you to continue our conversation. For each question, please check the most appropriate box.

	Uncomfortable	Comfortable	Totally Confident
How comfortable did you feel conducting virtual presentations prior to this Webinar?	☐	☐	☐
How comfortable do you feel now?	☐	☐	☐

	Definitely	In Most Cases	Never
Would your recommend this Webinar to a friend or business associate?	☐	☐	☐
Would you like us to contact you regarding other Webinars that our firm conducts?	☐	☐	☐

TABLE 27.1 (CONTINUED)

My full name:

My e-mail address:

My company:

My telephone number:

☐ I would like a PDF copy of this presentation (requires an e-mail address).

☐ I would like a call from a representative (requires a phone number).

Never End a Presentation with a Question-and-Answer Session

You need to end your presentation with an inspirational finale and a call to action. Nothing is more deflating than then a question-and-answer session. Try doing these throughout your session or early in your ending. I know that this sounds counterintuitive, but trust me: it works.

Be Helpful

Display your e-mail or Web address for at least 30 seconds toward the end of your presentation. This will convince attendees that you really do want them to contact you if they have any questions. Be sure to respond to any questions in 24 hours or less.

Disconnect Please

Ask all attendees to disconnect from the meeting, and make sure that they do so. Be very sure of this before you make any comments that you may regret later. People have lost good careers for not being careful about this.

REAL-WORLD EXAMPLE

At the conclusion of a presentation on the new health plan to all the Skyheart employees in one of your company's largest divisions, display headlines and statistics that support the importance of high-quality health insurance. Also highlight the percentage of workers who do not have health coverage, and challenges that all companies have in providing health coverage for their employees, while continuing to compete in an increasingly difficult economic climate with growing foreign competition.

Share or ask attendees to access the highlights of your new medical plan. Honestly review the benefits and differences in the new plan via audio. Ask participants to complete an online survey on their feelings about the new medical plan and the usefulness of your presentation.

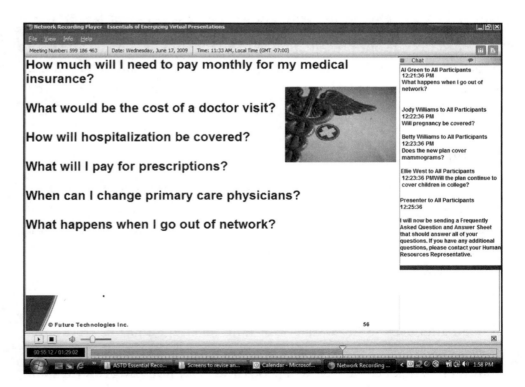

FIGURE 27.1: PRESENTING A NEW MEDICAL PLAN

Your producer/moderator will then ask you via audio several prearranged questions regarding common medical situations and how they will be handled by the new plan (see Figure 27.1). Answer these questions via audio or chat, and use the electronic whiteboard to summarize your answers.

Refer attendees to the frequently asked questions sheet that you can send them or that they can download. Also provide attendees with a resource or URL for gaining more information or asking questions.

Finally, thank participants for attending the session, for their valuable thoughts, and for their commitment as Skyheart employees.

TRY IT YOURSELF

Apply what you covered in this chapter to the presentation that you have been working on since Chapter 16 by using the spaces given to script the ending that you propose. Be sure to review the material in this chatper and Appendix F: Introduction and Summary Scripts and to include the following:

- Going back to why the attendees are here in the first place

- Conjuring up the hopes that the participants had at the beginning of the presentation

- Helping them imagine what it will feel like when they have successfully implemented the new skills, information, or attitudes embraced in your presentation

The Situation

Starion is about to make a major worldwide product introduction. In three months, it will begin taking orders for the Transporter 1000. The Transporter is the size of a microwave and can digitize and transport a small package from one point to another anywhere in the world, instantly. The Transporter is a completely new product class that has no competition.

The company would like you to conduct a series of virtual presentations to introduce the Transporter 1000 to its 1,000 direct salespeople and its top 3,000 distributors and channel partners. The goal of this effort is to enable personnel to position the benefits and features of the product and demonstrate its compelling usefulness.

As is the case with most revolutionary products, selling the Transporter 1000 will have its challenges. Among them is the price. The price of each unit will be $50,000, and Starion has been unsuccessful in the past in selling equipment at that high a price point.

Starion would like you to lead this effort by collaborating with the sales, marketing, and IT departments. Your management expects you to be the major presenter, but to also include regional sales managers and senior product managers as additional presenters. It expects these virtual presentations to take between 60 and 90 minutes and to utilize portions of presentations that have already been prepared by marketing, as well as several planned collaterals and Web pages.

You have been chosen for this important assignment because of your reputation as a quick learner and a gifted presenter. You are honored, but you are a bit nervous. You are new to conducting virtual presentations, and you have never conducted one of this magnitude.

Your Ending

_____

_____

_____

_____

_____

_____

_____

TROUBLESHOOTING VIRTUAL PRESENTATIONS

If anything can go wrong, it will.

—Murphy's Law

The premise of Murphy's Law is true with any new technology, and virtual presentations are no exception. Attendees may not be able to log in to your session, or your PowerPoint may not run the way you expect it to. There are also problems associated with your not being able to see your audience and them not being able to see you. Those problems are typically associated with attendees' wandering attention, such as checking e-mail or sending text messages during a session. As we all know, people do things in private that they would never do in public. Your attendees are no exception. They may leave the room and munch on a cookie, or they may feel comfortable having an irrelevant side conversation with another attendee at best, or engaging in a chat that is disrespectful to another attendee at worst. Virtual environments are an interesting blend of the public and the private, and they sometimes manifest the dysfunction of both. Thankfully, most of the time there will be a solution to whatever difficulty you come across in preparing or delivering a virtual presentation.

This section of the book will cover how to troubleshoot various situations that you might encounter:

Chapter 28: Handling Technical Problems

Chapter 29: Overcoming Silence and Resistance

Chapter 30: Controlling Your Audience

HANDLING TECHNICAL PROBLEMS

When you are dealing with computers and computer services, things can and do go wrong. Computers can freeze up, hard drives can crash, and communications can fail. Many such technical disasters can be anticipated, planned for, and guarded against, and if you have to deliver a virtual presentation, then a good rule of thumb to have is "better safe than sorry." Here are a few ways to do that.

ALWAYS HAVE A CONTINGENCY PLAN

Part of the planning process, as mentioned in an earlier chapter, is devising a contingency plan. Also set up two different computers, using separate Internet connections (e.g., data lines) and separate telephone lines (e.g., telephone numbers or extensions) for your virtual presentation. That way, if any one of those malfunctions, there will be a replacement ready to go.

A few ways to avoid technical problems before they happen is to verify attendees' computer environments and request that the attendees test the service, software, and communication lines before the day of your session. I also recommend conducting dry runs in your live environment with a few attendees online, to identify any additional technical issues. Do not forget to test your presentation, media, and links both prior to and on the day of your virtual presentations. Remember Murphy's Law—if there's a chance that it can fail, it just might. And of course, always arrange for a technical support person to be on hand the day of your virtual presentation.

Include an alternative way for participants to reach you and for you to reach them, such as calling cell phone numbers. Finally, always be ready to cut bait if the technology fails and conduct your presentation the old-fashioned way by e-mailing your PowerPoint slides and handouts and conducting the presentation as a teleconference.

PROFESSIONALISM IS NOT WHAT HAPPENS WHEN EVERYTHING GOES RIGHT

Professionalism is what happens when everything goes wrong. It is easy to shine when everything is working well. A true professional is one who can recover and save the day when circumstances are far less than perfect. Rehearse enough to be able to switch gears quickly without getting flustered, and take your flexibility pill in the morning. Be prepared to be intellectually agile during the presentation.

MOST PEOPLE WILL NOT NOTICE SMALL PROBLEMS

Thank goodness most people are too focused or too distracted to notice tiny glitches! Do not draw attention to small mistakes or problems. Just take a breath and move on. Use a transition statement such as, "next slide, please," and keep it moving. In most cases, your producer/moderator will cover for you by saying something like, "This will just take a minute" or, "Pardon me, but this may take some time; how about we come back to this later on." Never allow minor setbacks to deter you from reaching your goal.

WHAT CAN YOU DO WHEN THE SHOW CANNOT GO ON?

Sometimes there are reasons why you simply cannot go on, such as if a large number of attendees cannot log in to your virtual presentation, the PowerPoints that are the cornerstone of your session will not display, or key screens that you would like to share will not cooperate. After a moderate amount of effort to set things right doesn't work, sincerely apologize and indicate that you will contact attendees to reschedule. Most attendees will understand. Everyone has run into technical problems of her own at some time. Your attendees will appreciate a sincere apology and your willingness to reschedule your presentation, rather than wasting their time while you fumble around to no avail.

OVERCOMING SILENCE AND RESISTANCE

Attendees will not always be actively engaged in your presentation or committed to its success. They may be silent or even resistant to your session. They may feel overworked, resent their boss's making them attend your virtual presentation, or not feel positive about the message that you are about to share. Either way, it is up to you to overcome this potential silence and resistance as best you can without further upsetting them. Who knows, maybe you can transform them into believers. Here are some points to remember that might help you do so.

YOUR MOTHER WILL ALWAYS LOVE YOU

If you are fortunate, maybe you have a significant other, a dog, a cat, or a child that feels the same way. Attendees, on the other hand, are not under any contractual obligation to love you. They are attending your virtual presentation merely to meet their own needs, not yours. Often, they will exert only as much effort as is needed to achieve what they want. The rest is up to you. Sometimes it will not be easy, and other times it may be downright unfair.

ALWAYS ASSUME THAT ATTENDEES ARE MULTITASKING

When you talk to someone on the phone, there is the illusion that both parties are sitting still on the edge of their respective seats, engaged solely in the conversation at hand. It's best not to think that the other person might be knitting a scarf or fixing a sandwich, rather than devoting all her attention to you—even though chances are, that is what she's doing.

A virtual presentation works the same way. Your participants could be reading their latest sales report or answering e-mails instead of hanging on your every word. Sometimes they are attending only out of obligation to their boss, and most of the time they have something else on their mind. It is your job to get and keep them interested. Accept that you are not entitled to their undivided attention. You need to earn it. Earning attendees' attention might be the main topic of this book. If you have been with me so far, you have a better than even chance of connecting with the people who attend your session, motivating them out of their own self-interest, and drawing them into your virtual presentation. Once this process starts, it is contagious, and before you know it, you will have a group of people who are communicating and sharing. It's magic, but it takes practice. It is only a matter of time. Until then, though, just assume that everyone is also checking their e-mail.

MANY PEOPLE WILL HIDE IF THEY CAN

Remember elementary school. Some kids would sit in the back of the room, hoping that the teacher did not see them and would not call on them. It is the same way in virtual presentations. Quieter attendees hide from view, and they can do that very effectively. As adults, folks feel that they are entitled to be silent observers. If your presentation is a requirement, they may not have that option. First of all, work hard to make your virtual presentation relevant, economical, interactive, dynamic, and enjoyable. If that is not enough, try coming up with some positive ways to involve them, such as using the types of activities discussed in earlier chapters. You can also send an attendee a private note asking him for his valuable perspective. If these techniques do not work, let him be and move on to another attendee. If you are too aggressive in trying to draw out a specific participant, he will not be happy, and you can bet that this will be reflected on his session feedback form.

CONTROLLING YOUR AUDIENCE

In most cases, the attendees of a virtual presentation will all be adults (at least technically). Because of this, I always expect good manners from my audiences. While I will try to diffuse some childish behavior, I will not accept back-of-the-room chatter, heckling, insults, or general rudeness in either a face-to-face or a virtual environment. One way to avoid these poor manners is to set some ground rules at the beginning of your virtual presentations. Chapter 18 contains a sample listing of those rules.

Here are a few techniques that you may consider using in order to control this type of behavior.

USING A VIRTUAL HAND

You cannot walk over to a disruptive participant during a virtual presentation, but you can send her a private e-mail. This enables you to communicate with her on a personal level. It also avoids embarrassing her in front of her colleagues, which may well make her defensive and make the situation even worse. If a person continues to be disruptive, you can also restrict audience audio and chats so that only you can speak and chats are visible only by you and your producer/moderator. The particular method that you might select to invoke these restrictions differs for each virtual presentation service or application, though most applications do provide this functionality. Limiting who can speak may substantially alter the effectiveness of your presentation, so you want to do so only if it's absolutely necessary. You may even be able to impose these restrictions on only the rude attendee and not need to restrict all attendees. Check with your IT staff or virtual presentation provider. If an attendee is very disruptive and you cannot control him, I would ask my producer/moderator or technical person to disconnect the disruptive participant from the presentation. If the presentation is internal, I would consider speaking to my manager or contacting the participant's boss shortly after the session.

REDUCING OR ELIMINATING VIRTUAL CLASSROOM CHATTER

Just as in grade school or during face-to-face presentations, friends will tend to sit next to each other and engage in extraneous conversation. Well, this also happens during virtual presentations. Friends chat. Most of the time this is OK, although sometimes it may disturb the rest of the group and diminish the effectiveness of your virtual presentation. I recommend using the techniques identified earlier, such as sending the people involved a kind though direct personal e-mail. As before, if that doesn't work, consider using the virtual meeting tool itself to restrict attendees' abilities to chat with each other or eliminating the disruptive attendees from the presentation.

CUTTING OFF ATTENDEES WHO DOMINATE THE SESSION

Yes, this also happens during virtual presentations. Just as there are people who want to disappear, there are those who insist on dominating these events. Do as you would in a face-to-face environment. Send him a kindly worded e-mail, or ask your producer/moderator to be the heavy and do it on your behalf. If the participant continues dominating the session, send a more strongly worded e-mail. If all else fails, restrict the attendee's privilege to speak or to send chats to others. As before, if you are left with no other alternative, terminate him from the session. Yes, you can do that. Whenever you terminate an attendee from the session, I recommend that you communicate with those who invited this attendee, such as his manager or his sales account manager, immediately after the session, informing her of your decision and your willingness to include another member of her company or group in the next virtual session.

CONVERTING AN EXISTING PRESENTATION TO A VIRTUAL PRESENTATION

Imagination is more important than knowledge. For while knowledge defines all we currently know and understand, imagination points to all we might yet discover and create.

— Albert Einstein

To *conduct* a great virtual presentation, you first need to *create* a great virtual presentation. Although you may, of course, be called upon to develop a virtual presentation from scratch, you will often begin with an existing face-to-face presentation. One of the main points you should come away from this book with, and I can't emphasize this enough, is that almost anything you can do in a face-to-face presentation, you can also do in conducting a virtual presentation. The only element standing in your way is your own imagination.

CONVERTING AN EXISTING PRESENTATION TO A VIRTUAL PRESENTATION

This chapter covers the task of turning a preexisting face-to-face presentation into a great virtual presentation. It's important to keep in mind, though, that if the virtual version is to succeed, the face-to-face version will have to be serviceable already. Otherwise, you might as well start from scratch. If you do not have an existing face-to-face presentation or if the one that you do have is less than adequate, and you need to start from scratch, the hints and guidelines presented in this chapter should be of great help.

ANALYZE YOUR EXISTING PRESENTATION AND YOUR NEW AUDIENCE

I recommend that you initially sit down with your presentation and assets (e.g., handouts, Web links, and media) and create a presentation plan that clearly identifies what you intend to do, when you intend to do it, and what tools you will use. You might want to create your plan by filling out a virtual presentation planning form. Table 31.1 is one element of a completed plan that you could use as a place to begin.

Table 31.2 is a blank copy of the full virtual presentation planning form that you can use. Be sure to complete each row, since each represents one of the elements of a successful virtual presentation.

Customizing or creating a virtual presentation is more demanding than putting together a face-to-face one. In a face-to-face presentation, you have a great deal of social presence just by virtue of your being

TABLE 31.1 VIRTUAL PRESENTATION SNAPSHOT: CALMING IRATE CUSTOMERS

Element	Strategy	Tools	Assets
Present information	Discuss what strategies participants have found useful in the past.	Chat Polling	Stored chat and polling entries
	Take notes and clarify, enhance, or add to participants' comments to reflect the recommended steps for calming irate callers.	Electronic whiteboard	Stored whiteboard entries
	Distribute and summarize the techniques that your department would like your customer service agents to use.	Document sharing	Document: Steps in calming irate participants

TABLE 31.2 VIRTUAL PRESENTATION PLANNING FORM

Element	Strategy	Tools	Assets
Preparation and administration			
Gain attention and establish relevance			
Introduce yourself and others			
Identify objectives and set expectations			
Present information			
Conduct demonstrations			
Ask and answer questions			
Initiate and manage discussions			
Promote interaction			
Utilize assessments and evaluations			
End with a bang			

physically in the same room. Simply put, social presence is the degree to which each person is able to command the attention of others when he is communicating. Most people become presenters because they have a high degree of social presence. Many worry that their charisma will not translate into the virtual environment, and that is a very reasonable fear. Only a few great athletes make good radio hosts. The qualities that give them a commanding social presence on the field don't necessarily translate to the qualities it takes to hold a radio audience's attention.

One way to make up for the lack of social presence in virtual presentations is to have the right materials, so that you do not have to wing it and rely upon your charm. Having an outstanding presentation with valuable handouts takes the pressure off you. With high-quality materials, you don't have to perform with no net and rely upon your charm. Since this is not a book on creating blockbuster presentations, I won't give you my opinions on how you can come across as a magnetic force of nature in the personality department. Rather, I will simply provide you with guidelines for translating your successful face-to-face presentations into huge virtual successes.

Put Your Presentation on a Diet

As was strongly stated in previous chapters, virtual audiences will not tolerate a long presentation. I was shocked to learn that most major television national news stories are only 2 to $2\frac{1}{2}$ minutes long, with 30 seconds being allotted for local pieces. Strive to make your virtual presentation about 45 to 60 minutes long. By the way, do not make your presentation less than 20 minutes. Attendees tend to feel that anything less than 20 minutes is trivial and not worth their time.

Analyze Your Audience

Since you will not be able to make judgments on the fly, you will need to thoroughly analyze the people who will be attending your presentation beforehand. Will the size of your audience be changing? You need to know that so that you can adjust your presentation accordingly. You can incorporate more audio, flexibility, and collaboration with smaller audiences than you can with larger ones. With larger audiences, you commonly need to restrict attendees' ability to speak and to share chats with the rest of the group.

One way or another, you need to determine how many participants will attend, who they are, how the presentation is relevant to them, and their history with regard to the topic. Also, be very clear about what you would like attendees to do as a result of your presentation, such as buy a product or fix a software glitch. Regardless, focus your presentation primarily on what is most important to them, so that you can achieve the goal that is important to you.

DESIGN YOUR PRESENTATION

Here are some design decisions that you should probably make early in the game when you are planning to convert your in-person presentation into a virtual one.

- **To chat or not to chat?** With smaller audiences, you will probably want the warmth and partnership that come with speaking. When you are presenting to large audiences, you will appreciate the control that you have when you use chats. You or your producer/moderator can determine which chats you display and which questions you choose to answer. You may also decide to group questions and respond to them at a natural breaking point in your virtual presentation.

- **Who can talk with whom?** The United States is a democracy, and we typically believe in free speech and that all voices deserve to be heard. That works fine with small audiences. With larger audiences, however, it creates anarchy. In those cases, provide attendees with the ability to chat with you or the producer/moderator, but provide them with the ability to chat with other attendees only on a limited basis.

- **To YouTube or not to YouTube?** I personally love using YouTube videos. While you do need to be selective, YouTube contains a wealth of material on just about any topic that you can think of. There are a few problems with using content from this site, though. There are some utilities that you can use to copy the videos and run them from your computer or distribute them to attendees in a shared folder, but if you do so, be sure that you are not in violation of any copyright laws first. You may also stream the videos from the Web and then share your screen. Often the videos will run very slowly and choppily when you use this method. Finally, you may provide attendees with the YouTube link using the chat feature, but many corporate firewalls do not allow employees to access YouTube. My recommendation is that you decide on a couple of methods you would like to use early on, test them, and provide attendees with some options.

- **Webcams are an interesting idea, but can you really live with them?** You may be enticed by the ability of others to see your shining face, but do you also want them to see you reading your notes? Will you always look your professional best? Think about it. Also, existing Internet technology feeds from Webcams run painfully slowly. As Webcams get better and Internet connections faster, Webcams can be very useful in virtual presentations. If you do decide to use a Webcam, please review the guidelines and cautions that we have identified in previous chapters of this book.

- **Will more be merrier?** For larger and longer presentations, consider using one or more presenters, or even a panel. Be sure to provide, or quality assure, each presenter's materials. As best you can, make sure that the other presenters rehearse alone and that they participate in at least one dry run all together (virtually or face-to-face).

- **Where can you plan to be spontaneous?** Do you really think that Billy Crystal, Ellen DeGeneres, Jim Carrey, and Tina Fey do not work at being spontaneously funny? Well, think again! They do. You can seem spontaneous only when you are meticulously prepared. Sure, you can improvise from time to time, but only when you have a wealth of routines nailed down that you can draw upon at will. As an example, most late-night hosts have a wealth of prepared lines that they use when they fumble or when a joke falls flat on its face. If you pay attention, you will notice at least one of these events during every monologue. David Letterman recently handled a joke failing by saying, "Boy, this is a cold audience. Did you all come here from Saskatoon?" Every comedian has a wealth of seemingly spontaneous fallback lines to draw from in the event that one of his untested jokes doesn't go over well.

- **How can I get attendees to stick around until the end?** Hold back some useful material, such as a job aid, pocket chart, or timely article, and distribute it at the end of your presentation. Let attendees know that you will be doing this. Try to make this last-minute gift very "wow."

- **Where can I gather additional materials for my presentation?** You can find more materials for your presentation just about anywhere. These materials can include audio testimonials, quick yet professional video demonstrations, collaterals, and certainly graphics. In addition to using your existing presentations, I recommend that you speak with people in sales, product management, marketing, and a variety of other technical and corporate departments (e.g., human resources, safety, and facilities) for materials that are appropriate to your presentations.

DEVELOP YOUR PRESENTATION

With your new virtual presentation planning form and additional assets in hand, you can now begin revising your face-to-face presentation into a virtual presentation.

Here are a few activities that will make your virtual presentations resonate. While these activities are particularly critical when you convert a face-to-face presentation into a virtual presentation, they are useful in preparing and enhancing any presentation. For a variety of reasons, weaknesses in face-to-face presentations are not as apparent. Virtual presentations need to be tighter.

- **Increase the number of slides in your presentation.** Break up key points into individual slides, and find graphics that emphasize and complement your verbal presentation. Since you are not there in person, the more visual stimulation the viewers have to hold their attention, the better.

- **Use less text and more graphics in your PowerPoint slides.** Stop using your slides as an outline. Remember to design your PowerPoint slides so that they are visual and telegraphic. Instead of using the sentence, "The T1000 reduces the cost of ownership," use, "Reduced cost of ownership." Get over the feeling that you need to use full sentences. When you are creating or revising PowerPoints, your displays should look more like signs than like paragraphs. Remember that they are aids to your attendees, not a crutch for you. You can include talking points in your quick and dirty Presenter's Guide, which we will discuss later in this chapter.

- **Transfer detailed information to handouts.** Large amounts of text, data, graphs, URLs, or other reference information should be included in handouts that are separate from your presentation slide content. Make your presentation about the value and use of the data, not about the information itself. If a listener cannot actively use the data while listening to you, those data do not belong in the presentation.

- **Get rid of extraneous graphics and video.** Do not use cute visuals that are not critical to your message. As important as it is to hold your audience's attention, your video presentations should be more than just eye candy. A simple visual theme, such as a timeline, can be helpful. Make sure that the graphics or videos that you employ serve a purpose or get rid of them.

- **Reformat your slides to make them easy to read in a smaller area.** Use high-contrast colors that let the foreground text be easily seen and read over the background. The area in which your slides will be displayed in your virtual presentation is small, and your PowerPoint slides need to be completely readable.

- **Reorganize your presentation, placing the most important information up front.** Because virtual presentations tend to be shorter than face-to-face presentations, you should consider making sure that the most important points come early. Identify slides near the end of your presentation that you can skip if you are short on time. It is better to eliminate content than to rush through it in a panicked attempt to jam everything into a time slot. If you do elect to leave out information to meet your schedule, do not call attention to the fact. Let attendees think that you had always planned to deliver exactly as much material as they heard.

- **Remove distractions.** Small, subtle animations can be useful in focusing the audience's attention. For instance, you might use animation to add an arrow pointing to a key item on a slide. Avoid the temptation to add repetitive and distracting animations, such as text that flies in for each bullet point. You can also use annotation features in your Web conferencing software to draw lines, arrows, boxes, and other highlights that pull your audience's focus to the screen and synchronize their attention.

- **Do not make your attendees wish they had a pillow.** Sitting quietly and staying fully focused is tough enough in a face-to-face presentation under the gaze of all your colleagues. Doing so when you are alone with plenty of distractions is much harder. It's your job, as a presenter, to keep your attendees tuned in to what you are saying and following along. Add lots of interaction and variety to your presentation, so that your attendees don't switch the station, so to speak.

- **Plant and you will reap.** We have addressed this several time in other chapters, but this technique is useful enough to mention here. Prepare planted questions for each important topic. Your producer/moderator can use these questions to seed discussions and question-and-answer sessions.

- **Make life easy on yourself—*be prepared.*** There are a lot more ins and outs to a virtual presentation than to an in-person one, and you want to double-check to make sure that everything is squared away before you get started. Place copies of your media in one folder. Create files of polling questions, planted questions, and URLs labeled by when you will need them.

- **Create a quick and dirty Presenter's Guide.** Taken in total, this should be the shooting script for your presentation. It should include the following:

  ○ Handouts of your PowerPoint presentation with three slides to a page.

  ○ Talking points on the right-hand side where they are easy to see.

  ○ A completed virtual presentation planning form (see Appendix E for a blank form).

  ○ Carefully scripted notes for your introduction and ending. This will help you begin your presentation forcefully and end with a bang.

  Plan to update and simplify your guide as you gain more experience conducting your virtual presentation.

- **Lean toward the professional side.** If you will be using video, plan to make it more on the professional side. Even if you are using the video for a quick and dirty demonstration, such as a software demo, plan to edit it and include labels and directional elements (e.g., arrows and boxes). If you will be broadcasting yourself live, consider using a professional videographer and video setup and an enhanced location, instead of your computer Webcam.

PRODUCE YOUR VIRTUAL PRESENTATION

While we may have covered the production guidelines given here in other chapters, I feel that it is important to highlight the next two activities, since they are critical to successfully converting a face-to-face presentation to an effective virtual presentation.

- **Small can still be beautiful.** The presentation window on attendees' screens will be much smaller than the attendees are accustomed to in a meeting room or standard desktop presentation. To make sure that your presentation is still effective, you need to take a few precautions, including testing that *your presentation is readable when you resize the main slide area to 50 percent.*

- **Use simple backgrounds, fonts, and colors in your PowerPoints and other materials.** Complex backgrounds may look cool, but they distract attendees' attention. Too many fonts and colors begin to look amateurish. Stick to a couple of fonts and maybe three "related" colors. Use font sizes of 30 points or more. You may be able to go as low as 20 points in a pinch, but never below that. Do not use shadowed type styles. They do not translate well into most virtual meeting services and applications. Use labels and directional cues (e.g., arrows or boxes) discreetly and well. Simplify, simplify, and simplify some more. Do not use builds. The meaning of a click changes when you use a build. This increases your chances of making a mistake during the presentation itself. You can always fake a build by using multiple slides. Design the last one first, and then work backward by deleting selections.

VIRTUAL PRESENTATION CASE STUDY EXERCISE

I t is said that people learn best by example and by doing. In Part 5 of this book, we present a case study on developing and conducting a virtual presentation. We also provide you with a Take Action activity where you can begin working on a virtual presentation that you plan to conduct in the near future. We hope that this part of the book assists you in putting together all the things that we have covered in this comprehensive resource and helps you begin to apply the concepts, best practices, and guidelines that we have shared with you to virtual presentations of your own.

This portion of the book contains the following chapters:

Chapter 32: Putting It All Together

Chapter 33: Take Action

PUTTING IT ALL TOGETHER

For those of you who are brave, this chapter contains a case study exercise that you may wish to review. The objective of the virtual presentation is to present customer service personnel with a strategy for calming irate customers. Have you ever been there—on one side of the equation or the other? I am sure that we all have.

Table 32.1 is a virtual presentation snapshot for this presentation. It specifies the communications strategy, virtual presentation tools, and assets employed for each element of the presentation. Take a moment now to analyze this form to see how the various elements come together to create a compelling virtual presentation that yielded the solid business results of more satisfied customers, retaining accounts, and increasing the menu of products that customers have purchased from the company.

TABLE 32.1 VIRTUAL PRESENTATION SNAPSHOT: CALMING IRATE CUSTOMERS

Element	Strategy	Tools	Assets
Gain attention and establish relevance	Ask participants to consider how effective they have been in the past in reacting to irate callers.	Audio and polling	PowerPoint presentation and stored polling questions
	Play audio snippets of customer service personnel reacting to irate callers. Use samples in which service personnel were OK, but were just not able to turn the conversation around.	Media window Chat to distribute URLs	Audios of customers
	Conduct a discussion on what the agents could have done better.	Audio or chat and electronic whiteboard	Stored electronic whiteboard entries
Introduce yourself and others	Ask the producer/moderator to introduce you.	Audio	PowerPoint presentation
	Ask attendees to send you a picture of themselves and a description of a	E-mail and chat	Attendee photographs Prepared chat entries

TABLE 32.1 (CONTINUED)

Element	Strategy	Tools	Assets
	customer service event that made them extremely irate as a consumer. Request that they include something about themselves, such as their department and the types of customer issues that they are responsible for resolving. Use a prepared situation to get things rolling.		
	Ask participants to match each participant with the appropriate customer service event.	Electronic whiteboard	
Identify objectives and set expectations	Clearly identify how you will determine participants' active involvement in this virtual presentation by displaying a recorded chat session and identifying the participants who you feel were actively participating and those who were not.	Audio, chat, and screen sharing	PowerPoint presentation Recorded chat session Stored chat entries Planted questions and prepared responses

(Continued)

TABLE 32.1 (CONTINUED)

Element	Strategy	Tools	Assets
Present information	Discuss and expand on techniques that attendees have found useful in the past.	Audio, chat, and polling	PowerPoint presentation and stored polling questions Stored chat entries Stored electronic whiteboard entries
	Summarize and reword participants' comments to reflect the recommended steps for calming irate callers.	Electronic whiteboard Shared folder or electronic transmission	Document: Steps in calming irate participants Stored whiteboard entries Planted questions and prepared responses
Conduct demonstrations	Demonstrate the steps and techniques for calming irate callers.	Audio	PowerPoint and audio presentation
	Ask a few pairs of participants to do the same and have the group rate their performance.	Polling	Stored polling questions

TABLE 32.1 (CONTINUED)

Element	Strategy	Tools	Assets
Ask and answer questions	Ask attendees to describe any problems they see in using this technique.	Chat	Stored chat entries
	Conduct a discussion and summarize the results.	Electronic whiteboard	Stored electronic whiteboard entries
Initiate and manage discussions	Suggest that most of the time, irate callers create their own problems and deserve what they get.	Audio	PowerPoint presentation
	Ask participants if anyone agrees or disagrees with this, and why.	Chat/polling	Stored polling questions or chat entries
	Facilitate the discussion and use the whiteboard to note why irate callers may be irate and what they can, and should, expect from customer service personnel.	Audio and electronic whiteboard	Stored electronic whiteboard entries
Promote interaction	Separate attendees into pairs.	Audio Breakout rooms	

(Continued)

TABLE 32.1 (CONTINUED)

Element	Strategy	Tools	Assets
	Assign half of the attendees speaker roles and the others the role of the irate caller.	Audio, chat, or electronic whiteboard	
	Ask the speakers to recall the situation that made them extremely irate that they shared at the beginning of the virtual presentation. Ask them to describe the situation to their partner in more detail.	Audio or chat	
	Direct pairs to play out the role-play by directing the irate callers to tax the patience of the speakers and use whatever tactics they can to get the speakers to take their attacks personally. Explain that the goal of the speaker is to execute the process and not take the irate caller's comments to heart.	Audio Shared folder or electronically transmitted document	Stored role-playing instructions

TABLE 32.1 (CONTINUED)

Element	Strategy	Tools	Assets
	Bring pairs into the larger group and ask a couple of pairs to describe the results of the exercise, including who succeeded and why, and which portions of the technique worked and which did not.	Audio or chat and electronic whiteboard	Stored chat and whiteboard entries
Utilize assessments and evaluations	Ask participants to view a video presentation of customer service personnel attempting to employ the technique, rate each one on a scale of 1 to 10 on her successful execution of the technique, and identify areas that are in need of improvement.	Media window Electronic whiteboard	Media showing agents employing the technique well, poorly, and somewhere in the middle
	Review and summarize the results.	Polling	Stored polling questions
End with a bang	Ask attendees to recall their worst experience handling irate customers and	Audio or chat	PowerPoint presentation Stored chat entries

(Continued)

TABLE 32.1 (CONTINUED)

Element	Strategy	Tools	Assets
	describe how this technique could have helped.		
	Encourage attendees to complete a short feedback form.	Shared folder or electronically transmitted document	Stored electronic feedback form
	Display statistics on the level of customer satisfaction in their industry and how these statistics correspond to renewal rates.	Media window	PowerPoint presentation Stored statistics document
	Request that attendees commit to reviewing the technique presented every Friday at 4:45 for at least a month. Ask attendees to send you a short e-mail if they have the opportunity to use the technique to let you know how it worked out.	Audio	PowerPoint presentation
	Present your contact information and thank attendees for their time.	Audio	PowerPoint presentation Stored contact information

TABLE 32.1 (CONTINUED)

Element	Strategy	Tools	Assets
	Indicate that you will remain online to answer questions.		
	At the end of the questions, log off of the virtual meeting service or application.		
After the presentation	Edit the virtual presentation and post it.	Virtual presentation service or application	Edited virtual presentation
	Respond to participant questions that you offered to research.	E-mail	
	Send thank-you notes to attendees, remind them of their follow-up commitment, and restate your offer to continue to help.	E-mail or virtual presentation service or application	Thank-you note
	Make enhancement notes for future presentations.		Presentation diary
	Prepare and present a report to your management.	Virtual presentation service or application	Management report

TAKE ACTION

Now, use the information that you have gleaned from this book to plan a virtual presentation that you expect to be presenting in the near future.

STEP 1

Use the virtual presentation preparation form in Table 33.1. For instructions on how to complete this form, refer to Chapter 15.

TABLE 33.1 TAKE ACTION: VIRTUAL PRESENTATION PREPARATION FORM

Element	Activity	Resource	Due Date
Preparation and administration	**A month prior to the presentation**		
	Complete the virtual presentation preparation form.		
	Schedule the presentation.		
	Select team members and assign roles.		
	Finalize contracts with outside resources.		
	Select a title and write a description of your presentation.		
	Prepare the virtual presentation, autoplay, and associated materials.		
	Prepare all presenters.		
	Promote the presentation.		
	Ensure that the appropriate personnel, facilities, and technology are available.		
	Collaborate with other departments.		
	Create a registration page.		
	Communicate with attendees.		

(Continued)

TABLE 33.1 (CONTINUED)

Element	Activity	Resource	Due Date
	A week prior to the presentation		
	Send an e-mail reminder.		
	Review and refine your presentation materials.		
	Check the rooms.		
	Select your wardrobe.		
	Create or acquire a participant list.		
	Upload supporting materials.		
	Conduct solo and group rehearsals.		
	A day before the presentation		
	Send another e-mail reminder.		
	Conduct a dry run.		
	Verify all applications, Web links, and media.		
	Cleanse your automatic browser entries.		
	Select an appropriate screen size.		
	The day of the presentation		
	Keep things calm.		
	Send a short e-mail reminder.		

TABLE 33.1 (CONTINUED)

Element	Activity	Resource	Due Date
	Test everything again.		
	Take care of your voice.		
	An hour before the presentation		
	Send a final e-mail reminder.		
	Gather your materials.		
	Log on to your computer.		
	Log on to a second computer connected to a second line.		
	Begin your autoplay presentation.		
	Turn off cell phone, e-mail, instant messaging, and pop-ups.		
	Mute computer.		
	Shut down unneeded applications.		
	Keep a glass of water at room temperature nearby.		
	Place and adjust headset.		
	Immediately prior to the presentation		
	Begin your pre-presentation routine.		

(*Continued*)

TABLE 33.1 (CONTINUED)

Element	Activity	Resource	Due Date
	Arrive at your presentation site 30 minutes beforehand.		
	Log on to your presentation 15 minutes early.		
	Greet each attendee by name.		
	Ask questions to show that you are interested.		
	Immediately following your presentation		
	Send attendees a thank-you e-mail.		
	Distribute promised materials to attendees.		
	Edit and store your presentation.		
	Send materials to nonattending registrants.		
	Make sure your sales department follows up within 24 hours.		
	Send out a brief survey to attendees.		
	Provide attendees with reasons to return to your Web site or to a follow-on presentation.		

TABLE 33.1 (CONTINUED)

Element	Activity	Resource	Due Date
	Make enhancement notes for future presentations.		
	Prepare and present a report to your management.		

STEP 2

Script the introduction that you would like your producer/moderator to use in introducing you. Use the blanks given here.

_____

_____

_____

_____

_____

_____

STEP 3

Now plan the remainder of your own presentation, using the blank virtual presentation planning form in Table 33.2. If you need some help, refer to the job aid in Appendix A or the book itself.

SUMMING IT UP

Organizations are seeking inexpensive ways to operate faster, reduce expenses, and reach out to a continuously widening global market. Virtual meetings are a wondrous method for accomplishing this feat. But not all virtual meetings will get the job done; only those that are compelling,

TABLE 33.2 VIRTUAL PRESENTATION PLANNING FORM

Element	Strategy	Tools	Assets
Preparation and administration			
Gain attention and establish relevance			
Introduce yourself and others			
Identify objectives and set expectations			
Present information			
Conduct demonstrations			
Ask and answer questions			
Initiate and manage discussions			
Promote interaction			
Utilize assessments and evaluations			
End with a bang			
After the presentation			

interactive, and engaging will do it. We firmly believe that anything that you can do in a face-to-face meeting, you can replicate in a virtual meeting. And with the powerful tools incorporated in modern virtual presentation services and applications, you may even be able to do a good bit more.

The purpose of this book was to ensure your success by preparing you to develop and deliver rich virtual presentations that audiences will gladly attend and will not forget. These presentations may include sales meetings, product launches, technical seminars, product demonstrations, company briefings, training courses, impromptu speeches, panels, and roundtables. We fully expect that after reading this book, your virtual presentations will increase your organization's sales and operating efficiency, and, of course, your own success.

Happy trails, and I wish you the best of luck prospering in our increasingly virtual world.

MAKING EFFECTIVE VIRTUAL PRESENTATIONS JOB AID

PREPARATION AND ADMINISTRATION (CHAPTER 11)

One Month before the Presentation

- Managing it all:

    - Arranging, preparing, and conducting a large virtual presentation requires the flawless execution of a multitude of activities.

    - Solicit assistance and assign roles and responsibilities.

    - Create a project plan.

- Schedule your presentation.

- Prepare your presentation.

- Prepare yourself and the other presenters.

- Promote your presentation.

- Ensure that appropriate personnel, facilities, and technology are available.

- Collaborate with other departments.

- Communicate with attendees.

PREPARATION AND ADMINISTRATION (CHAPTER 12)

One Week before the Presentation

- Send a motivating e-mail reminder.

- Review and refine your presentation materials.

- Check the room where you will be conducting the event.

- Select your wardrobe.

- Create a list of participants, including their usernames and passwords.

- Upload supporting materials.

- Rehearse!

PREPARATION AND ADMINISTRATION (CHAPTER 13)

One Day before the Presentation

- Send another e-mail reminder.

- Conduct a dry run of your presentation.

- Verify everything technical:

  - Verify that all applications, Web links, and media presentations are working as expected.

  - Ensure that all participants have access to the prepared resources and that the virtual meeting area is up and running.

  - Confirm the readiness of participants' equipment and the resources used during the presentation.

  - Ensure that all presenter and attendee materials, such as presentation media, participant materials, and presenter materials, are loaded or in a separate folder ready to transmit.

  - Log on as a participant to ensure that the participants will be viewing what you expect them to view.

  - Cleanse your automatic browser entries or have a browser that you use only for virtual presentations.

  - Set an appropriate screen size.

PREPARATION AND ADMINISTRATION (CHAPTER 14)

The Morning of the Presentation

- Keep things calm.

- Send a short e-mail reminder.

- Conduct a final test of your Internet connection, virtual meeting service or application, presentation, media, and materials.

- Avoid dairy products, caffeine, and smoking, and prepare a glass of water at room temperature.

An Hour before Your Presentation

- Send a final e-mail reminder.

- Gather your materials.

- Begin a media-rich and compelling autoplay presentation.

- Log on as a participant, as well as a presenter.

- Turn off cell phones and mobile devices.

- Mute your computer sound and shut down unnecessary applications.

- Disable pop-ups and instant messaging.

- If you have two telephone lines, make sure that the second line does not ring during your presentation.

- Place and adjust your headsets.

Immediately prior to Your Presentation

- Begin your pre-presentation routine.

- Arrive at the area where you will be conducting your presentation at least 30 minutes early.

- Start your session at least 15 minutes early and greet each attendee by name. Use audio or polling to ask attendees about themselves and how they hope to benefit from your virtual presentation.

PREPARATION AND ADMINISTRATION (CHAPTER 15)

During Your Presentation

- Remember to breathe and breathe deeply.

- Consider using an attention meter.

- When you use screen sharing, ask attendees to let you know when they begin seeing your screen and if they are experiencing delays in watching media presentations.

- Make technical facts more interesting by adding explicit statements of their value.

- Avoid scrolling quickly.

- If you click on something, explain what you are clicking on.

- Be sure to speak slowly and clearly.

- Avoid statements such as "look over here" or "notice this." Instead, use statements such as "look at the second bullet of the screen" or "notice the arrow at the top left-hand corner of your screen."

- Be very careful before your press the Send button.

- Paint pictures with your words.

- Vary your intonations. This includes your pitch, volume, and inflections.

- Note attendees' names and use them as much as you can.

- Sustain a fast and lively pace that might seem just a bit faster than is comfortable for the average participant.

- Smile, even if the attendees cannot see you.

- Avoid statements like "I hope this works."

- Use the singular "you" in your statements and questions.

- Instead of saying, "I wonder if anyone out there can answer this question," say, "I wonder if you know the answer to this question?"

- Where appropriate, include support information such as Web resources and an e-mail box for questions to subject matter experts (SMEs).

- Include an "I didn't know that" whiteboard.

- Expect that unexpected things will happen.

- Psychologically prepare yourself to be flexible, agile, and intellectually nimble.

- Avoid distributing all of your handouts at the beginning of your presentation. Wait until the participants need them.

- Include contact information in your handouts.

- Send private messages to attendees complimenting them on their chats and other involvement in your virtual presentation, and chat messages to participants whom you feel need extra help or encouragement.

Immediately Following Your Presentation

- Send an e-mail to each attendee, thanking him for coming and recognizing his contribution.

- Follow up on unanswered participant questions using e-mail, blogs, or an online forum. Distribute copies of the presentation, reference information, or other collaterals.

- Consider sending registrants who did not attend the same materials that you send to attendees, as well as a link to the recorded presentation.

- Contact registrants who did not attend. Invite them to view the recording or register for another upcoming Web seminar.

- If your virtual presentation is a sales vehicle, have the sales department contact participants no more then 24 hours after your presentation.

- Send a survey to participants, or use a survey service to make sure that the attendees received what they expected from your presentation.

- Prepare a report to your management demonstrating the value of your virtual presentation.

- Send attendees something useful resulting from the presentation, such as a handy job aid.

- Edit and post your presentation for attendees and those that were not able to attend.

GAINING ATTENTION AND ESTABLISHING RELEVANCE (CHAPTER 16)

- Never begin a presentation by having attendees introduce themselves.

- Begin with a strong introduction.

- Demonstrate that your presentation will be different.

- Use stories, current events, cartoons, movies, newspaper articles, or television clips.

INTRODUCING YOURSELF AND OTHERS (CHAPTER 17)

- Ask your producer/moderator to introduce you.

- Try innovative methods for introducing participants.

- Use polling to find out information about attendees.

- Use the chat feature to share audioconferencing details and other instructions that attendees need if they are to participate effectively in your virtual presentation.

IDENTIFYING OBJECTIVES AND SETTING EXPECTATIONS (CHAPTER 18)

- Have your producer/moderator review and demonstrate the basics of how to use the virtual meeting tools and provide attendees with some practice.

- Provide the objectives of the presentation without calling them objectives.

- Share the agenda and format of the meeting.

- If your session is longer than one hour, plan for a break or interactive activity every 50 minutes.

- Ask for audience feedback on how everything is working.

- Present the contingency plan in case the virtual meeting service or application fails.

- Ground rules in a virtual presentation may cover:

  - Do not call in from a cell phone.

  - Turn off other office phones and cell phones.

  - Do not place this call on hold; place the call on mute when you are not speaking.

  - Disable call waiting and instant messaging and e-mail alerts.

  - Close down all software that will not be used during the presentation, including instant messaging.

  - Be patient and do not speak on top of each other. Identify yourself when speaking. Speak clearly

  - Reduce distractions (e.g., barking dogs or TVs in other rooms).

  - Close your door.

- Do not use speakerphones or microphones; use a telephone or USB headset.

- Do not send or respond to e-mails. (This may be more enticing in virtual presentations, since the presenter cannot see the attendees, and they are already using their computers.)

- Ask questions. Participate actively in chats.

- Be courteous. Avoid side conversations with colleagues. Do not send private chat messages to other participants once the session starts.

PRESENTING INFORMATION (CHAPTER 19)

Use Strong Presentation Strategies

- Never be the "sage on the stage." Always attempt to be the "guide on the side."

- Use case studies or stories to engage participants.

- Frequently switch between different types of content delivery.

- Present key ideas using different types of media, including text, graphics, animations, illustrations, diagrams, schematics, and models.

- Keep in mind that excessive animation can be distracting and that lengthy text is difficult to read on the screen.

- Use additional presentation strategies that include simulations, analogies, case studies, examples, nonexamples, mnemonics, jokes, war stories, and testimonials.

- Present information from another point of view.

- Add supporting photographs or other media.

- Present information in a video format when you need to conduct a live demonstration or include a message from senior management or other company leaders.

- If you do use a Webcam, ensure the quality of video transmission.

Focus on the Delivery

- Present information in short chunks and in a logical flow.

- Address the most important issues on the presentation outline first, and do not review them for those who arrive late.

- Use the schedule you presented in the beginning throughout the presentation to reinforce concepts and assess the group's progress.

- Always finish on time, even if you have not covered all the material.

- Set the tone of the presentation, using the informality or formality of your postings, chats, stored standard responses, and e-mails.

- Deliver the content naturally.

- Vary the pace and format of the presentation every five or six minutes.

- Maintain a brisk pace.

- Use pregnant pauses and repeat key phrases.

- Increase the level of interaction and frequency of comprehension checks if there is very little visual feedback from participants.

- Give attendees clear signposts to organize their thinking.

- Provide content summaries throughout the session, or assign this task to participants.

- Solicit feedback frequently to make sure that participants are "with you."

- "Tell attendees what you are going to tell them; tell them; and then tell them what you have told them."

Use Your Tools Wisely

- Use the whiteboard as you would a flipchart to trigger visual memory.

- Point to, highlight, draw, and notate application screens.

- Enable participants to download documents from a shared folder.

- Ask attendees to refer to Web sites and other resources by pasting the Web site's URL into a chat.

- Consider several factors in deciding whether you will be using audio or chat for any activity or topic.

Test Everything and Recover Well

- Assess the quality of audio and video transmission by polling participants to determine if they can hear and see properly.

- If there are distractions as you are presenting, let participants know what is occurring.

- Do not show anger, and breathe when you feel yourself getting irritated.

CONDUCTING DEMONSTRATIONS (CHAPTER 20)

- Make your demonstrations simple.

- Keep your demonstrations "real."

- Make your demonstrations come alive.

- Ensure that your demonstrations are easy to follow.

- Get your audience involved.

- Do not forget to recognize participants for their contributions.

ASKING AND ANSWERING QUESTIONS (CHAPTER 21)

Answering Questions

- Early in the game, decide how you would like to handle questions from the audience.

- Repeat each question before you answer it.

- Ask investigative questions that will enable the participants to answer the question themselves.

- Do not feel that you have to be the one to answer every question.

- When you do not know the answer, admit it and offer to investigate.

Asking Questions

- Instruct participants to put a symbol (e.g., a raised hand or check mark) by their name when they are ready to answer one of your questions.

- Ask questions that can be answered via audio, chat, or writing on the electronic whiteboard.

- Request that participants construct summaries of new information, apply information in real-world scenarios, or answer "what-if" questions.

- Allow attendees time to think about the question.

- Use the chat and whiteboard features to ask and answer questions.

- Manage silence effectively during questioning periods.

INITIATING AND MANAGING DISCUSSIONS (CHAPTER 22)

Strategy 1: Initiate the discussion in a thought-provoking manner.

Strategy 2: Structure the discussion.

Strategy 3: Control the flow of the discussion.

Strategy 4: Provoke respectful controversy.

Strategy 5: Help participants listen to one another.

Strategy 6: Bring together diverse threads into a summary.

Strategy 7: Thank all participants for their contributions.

Practical Hints

SET UP OR PROVOKE THE DISCUSSION

- Open the discussion with a provoking comment by stating the specific outcomes that you expect from the discussion or by asking participants to review those more specific outcomes listed in a document in the shared folder.

- Give participants roles during discussions.

MANAGE THE DISCUSSION

- Structure the discussion by including a proposed outline of the discussion.

- Closely manage the discussion by asking another colleague to help you monitor the activity.

- Use the microphone, whiteboard, chat window, or e-mail to keep the discussion on track.

- Deal with disruptive participants quickly and kindly, using private chat postings or e-mails to help them see how they are coming across to others.

- Resolve differences of opinion by encouraging participants to explore and identify outside resources.

Keep the Discussion Moving

- Plant ideas by asking a leading question on the whiteboard or displaying it in the chat window.

- Help participants listen to each other by providing summary comments that explicitly reference participants' comments.

- Encourage diverse viewpoints.

- Draw out participants who seem to be missing the discussion by initially using private chat postings or e-mail to ensure that they are not having technology or skill problems.

Summarize the Discussion

- Bring together diverse threads into a summary by weaving together attendees' comments and connecting participants' contributions to the theme of the discussion.

- Always end the discussion by restating the goals of the discussion, summarizing the results, and relating the results to the next topic.

Promote Interaction during the Discussion

- Begin the discussion with a vague question and ask the audience members to further refine the question, answer it, and then identify why they made the choices that they did.

- Separate a discussion into separate questions and assign each question to one of several groups. At the conclusion, conduct a group discussion that ties together the various groups' contributions.

PROMOTING INTERACTION (CHAPTER 23)

- Polling is a good first step.

- Plan your interactive activities, fine-tune them, and practice them until they are predictably fantastic.

- Imagine how you will promote interaction.

- Use planted questions to get things started.

- Try using three attendees for interactive activities, rather then two.

- Summarize instructions for interactive activities on the electronic whiteboard.

- Do not expect 100 percent participation in the polls.

UTILIZING ASSESSMENTS AND EVALUATIONS (CHAPTER 24)

When to Use Assessments

- Use knowledge checks frequently during the presentation to check for understanding.

How to Use Assessments Wisely

- Include enough time in your presentation schedule to incorporate assessments.

- Ask questions that are clear, pertinent, brief, and challenging.

- Provide feedback that is clear, timely, relevant, and specific.

- Avoid feedback that is brief or abrupt.

Types of Questions That You Can Use

- Utilize true/false or multiple-choice questions.

- Include questions with a degree of difficulty that matches the audience's level of knowledge.

Try Something New

- Use fun assessment activities, such as games and simulations.

- Ask attendees to type as many words as come to mind about the topics included in the presentation, using the electronic whiteboard.

- Incorporate interactions where attendees need to identify the difference between something that is done well and something that is done not so well.

- Consider using an attention meter.

- Use additional question-and-answer tools, such as Adobe Breeze Presenter, for more robust assessments and evaluations.

How to Make Using Assessments and Evaluations Easier for You

- Have groups use materials and assessment instruments that are located in a shared folder or have them readily available to transmit.

- Do not feel the need to interpret the results of a poll. Have your producer/moderator do it or draw upon the expertise of the group.

- When you are presenting to a large audience, request that attendees respond using the chat tool, and respond to only a few key questions.

STRATEGIES FOR CREATING EXCITEMENT AND MOTIVATION (CHAPTER 25)

Eight Strategies for Getting People Fired Up

Strategy 1: Know your audience.

Strategy 2: Use a wide variety of presentation activities and media.

Strategy 3: Foster collaboration.

Strategy 4: Build relationships.

Strategy 5: Use discovery techniques.

Strategy 6: Be prepared for anything.

Strategy 7: Establish and maintain an exciting environment.

Strategy 8: Use interactive and attendee-delivered lectures.

ENDING WITH A BANG (CHAPTER 27)

- It is far better to leave your audience hungry for more than overwhelmed or bored with having received too much.

- Never end a presentation with a question-and-answer session or a feedback form.

- Think very hard about what type of feedback you really need and keep your feedback form brief.

- Display your e-mail or Web address for at least 30 seconds toward the end of your presentation.

- Be available for questions or comments at the end of the presentation.

- Make sure that all attendees disconnect from the meeting.

HANDLING TECHNICAL PROBLEMS (CHAPTER 28)

- Always have a contingency plan.

- Rehearse enough to be agile.

- Don't even mention small technical errors.

- Cut bait and reschedule if you simply cannot go on.

OVERCOMING SILENCE AND RESISTANCE (CHAPTER 29)

- Give participants time to respond. After a reasonable pause, rephrase the question or direct it to a specific participant.

- Provide your producer/moderator or a shill in the audience with prepared answers just to get the ball rolling.

VIRTUAL PRESENTATION PREPARATION FORM

Element	Activity	Resource	Due Date
Administration and preparation	**A month prior to the presentation** Complete the virtual presentation preparation form. Schedule the presentation. Select team members and assign roles. Finalize contracts with outside resources. Select a title and write a description of your presentation.		

(*Continued*)

Element	Activity	Resource	Due Date
	Prepare the virtual presentation, autoplay, and associated materials.		
	Prepare all presenters.		
	Promote the presentation.		
	Ensure that the appropriate personnel, facilities, and technology are available.		
	Collaborate with other departments.		
	Create a registration page.		
	Communicate with attendees.		
	A week prior to the presentation		
	Send an e-mail reminder.		
	Review and refine your presentation materials.		
	Check the rooms.		
	Select your wardrobe.		
	Create or acquire a participant list.		
	Upload supporting materials.		
	Conduct solo and group rehearsals.		
	A day before the presentation		
	Send another e-mail reminder.		
	Conduct a dry run.		
	Verify all applications, Web links, and media.		
	Cleanse your automatic browser entries.		
	Select an appropriate screen size.		

Element	Activity	Resource	Due Date
	The day of the presentation		
	Keep things calm.		
	Send a short e-mail reminder.		
	Test everything again.		
	Take care of your voice.		
	An hour before the presentation		
	Send a final e-mail reminder.		
	Gather your materials.		
	Log on to your computer.		
	Log on to a second computer connected to a second line.		
	Begin your autoplay presentation.		
	Turn off cell phone, e-mail, instant messaging, and pop-ups.		
	Mute computer.		
	Shut down unneeded applications.		
	Keep a glass of water at room temperature nearby.		
	Place and adjust headset.		
	Immediately prior to the presentation		
	Begin your pre-presentation routine.		
	Arrive at your presentation site 30 minutes beforehand.		
	Start your presentation 15 minutes early and begin your autoplay presentation.		

(Continued)

Element	Activity	Resource	Due Date
	Greet each attendee by name.		
	Ask questions to show that you are interested.		
	Immediately following your presentation		
	Send attendees a thank-you e-mail.		
	Distribute promised materials to attendees.		
	Edit and store your presentation.		
	Send materials to nonattending registrants.		
	Make sure your sales department follows up within 24 hours.		
	Send out a brief survey to attendees.		
	Provide attendees with reasons to return to your Web site or to a follow-on presentation.		
	Make enhancement notes for future presentations.		
	Prepare and present a report to your management.		

SAMPLE INVITATION

Dear Sales Executive,

Do not miss tomorrow's Webinar, sponsored by Future Technologies at 11 a.m. Eastern Standard Time.

Every company is seeking inexpensive ways to operate faster and more effectively, reduce expenses, and reach out to a continuingly widening global marketplace. So how do managers and executives do all of that without decreasing quality, customer satisfaction, and employee morale? More and more they are relying upon virtual meetings.

Regrettably, these presentations tend to be even more boring and less effective than face-to-face presentations. Do not let this stop you. Virtual presentations can be compelling, interactive, and engaging. This takes some time and effort, though not all that much. This is why you are reading this book.

The presentation will help you develop and deliver rich virtual presentations that your audience will not forget. Such compelling presentations can increase sales, reduce employee time to competency, and increase the adoption of key corporate initiatives.

To register, visit http://www.fttraining.com/.

Dr. Joel Gendelman
Future Technologies
Joel@FTtraining.com
303.979.1129 (Telephone)
831.618.9090 (Fax)
Joel Gendelman (Skype)
www.FTtraining.com

LISTING OF COMMON EMOTICONS

Emoticon	Meaning
:) or :-) or :^) or =) or B) or 8) or c8 or cB or :]	Example of eye/face variations of emoticons
:)	Smiley
;) or *)	Wink
X(	Pouty face
:(or 8c or Bc or B(or |8c or |8C or :[	Frown
:P or :p	Tongue sticking out, or blowing a raspberry (less commonly,:Þ /:b)

(Continued)

Emoticon	Meaning
:O	Surprise/shock
:/ *or:*\ *or* 8/ *or* 8\ *or* >/ *or* >\	Skeptical/annoyed/uneasy
:|	Expressionless/indifference/disappointment
xP *or* XP	Disgust/dead/straining/Mischievous
xD *or* XD	Laughing hard
:S *or* :s *or* ^o)	Confusion/crazy
:3	Cute/catlike behavior
:X *or:* #	Sealed lips/embarrassment
:-*	Kiss on the cheek
>:O *or* XO	Angry/yelling
>:(*or* >[	Angry/grumpy
>:) *or* }:)	Devious
0:)	Innocence/halo/angel
<3	Heart/love
</3	Broken heart
:'(*or:*,(*or:*_(*or:**(*or:*. . .(	Shedding a tear
@}->—	Rose
<:}	An emoticon to explain nothing

VIRTUAL PRESENTATION SNAPSHOT

Element	Strategy	Tools	Assets
Preparation and administration			
Gain attention and establish relevance			

Element	Strategy	Tools	Assets
Introduce yourself and others			
Identify objectives and set expectations			
Present information			
Conduct demonstrations			
Ask and answer questions			

(Continued)

Element	Strategy	Tools	Assets
Initiate and manage discussions			
Promote interaction			
Utilize assessments and evaluations			
End with a bang			
After the presentation			

INTRODUCTION AND SUMMARY SCRIPTS

NEW PRODUCT INTRODUCTION

Introduction

For the last two years, our competitors have been eating our lunch in the research and development space. They have been eroding our customer base by wowing people with their feeds and speeds. Finally, our laboratory in Japan has developed new technology that not only beats them at their own feeds and speeds game, but provides our high-capacity research and development customers with unparalleled value: twice the speed at half the cost.

During this short virtual presentation, I and a couple of the product managers will present this new technology and its associated products. We will also provide you with materials that will document our claims and their value. You have probably chosen to take part in this virtual presentation because you recognize our company's superior customer service and reliability. Now I am about to convince you of our technical prowess and how we can exponentially increase the return on your investment.

Now, before we go on, please share some important information with me by sending me a chat message. If you could realize your fondest dream for virtual storage in your organization, what would that be?

Summary

Thank you all for attending this virtual presentation. I hope that I was able to convince you of the value and benefits of this important step forward for Hatsi. Within the next 24 hours, you will receive a call from your account manager, who will speak with you in more detail about our newest technology and how it can provide increased value for you and your organization. Please take a moment now to note what you find most compelling about our new technology, how using our suite of new products would provide value to your organization, and what detailed information you would find helpful in making a decision to integrate this new technology into your virtual storage system.

Thank you very much for your time. My e-mail address is myemail@mycompany.com. I will be sending you a short evaluation sheet. Please answer the questions frankly. They are just for me and will not be shared with anyone else. And, of course, kindly contact me if you have any questions now or in the future.

Please disconnect from this presentation, or remain on the presentation to ask our product managers more detailed questions.

* * *

FINANCIAL SERVICES

Introduction

We have probably seen more change in our industry in the past two years than in the previous twenty. Home ownership continues to be a dream of most Americans, but the current financial climate has made it more difficult than ever to secure a home loan.

That was before, and now is after. In cooperation with the federal government, we will be aggressively rolling out a new type of home loan to first-time buyers. These loans will be safe, secure, competitive, and backed by the financial commitment of our great nation.

But before I go on, what is the biggest challenge facing new buyers in today's market?

Send me a chat with a description of a few "well-qualified" buyers whom you have recently worked with who were not able to secure a loan. Why? What would have helped them?

Summary

Thank you all for attending this virtual presentation. I hope I was able to convince you that our new loans can meet the needs of many of your buyers who could not previously qualify for a home loan. Please take this opportunity to download the Frequently Asked Question Sheet, if you have not already done so.

Before the end of the day, you will receive a call from one of our representatives, who will speak with you in more detail about this new loan program. Please take a moment now to note any buyers whom you are currently working with who would be interested in this type of loan product and what detailed information you would find helpful.

Thank you very much for your time. My e-mail address is myemail@mycompany.com. I will be sending you a short evaluation sheet. Please answer the questions frankly.

Kindly take this opportunity to disconnect from this presentation.

* * *

AVOIDING INDUSTRIAL ACCIDENTS

Introduction

These days, you do not hear much about industrial accidents. They are rare. How many of you would agree with that statement?

Do you recall any industrial accidents within the past 11 years? Here are a few that you may have forgotten.

October 23, 1989: Phillips disaster. An explosion and fire killed 23 and injured 314 in Pasadena, Texas.

May 13, 2000: Enschede fireworks disaster. A fire and explosion at a fireworks depot in Enschede, Netherlands, left 22 people dead.

March 23, 2005: Texas City refinery explosion. An explosion occurred at a British Petroleum refinery in Texas City, Texas. It is the third largest refinery in the United States and one of the largest in the world, processing 433,000 barrels of crude oil per day and accounting for 3 percent of the nation's gasoline supply. Over 100 were injured, and 15 were confirmed dead.

April 18, 2007: Qinghe Special Steel Corporation disaster. A ladle holding molten steel separated from the overhead iron rail, fell, tipped, and killed 32 workers, injuring another 6.

February 7, 2008: The 2008 Georgia sugar refinery explosion in Port Wentworth, Georgia, United States. A dust explosion at a sugar refinery killed 13 people and injured 42 others.

As a maintenance technician, you will be working with several systems that incorporate chemicals that can kill you. They include sulfuric acid and ammonia. Our job today is to make sure that you are not one of those statistics.

This is about as much as I want to talk during this virtual presentation. I am more interested in showing you the dangers in your environment and demonstrating the precautions that you can take to make sure that you return from work safely. I do not think that I am the only smart one in the room, and I look forward to your help and experience in learning from each other.

Most of us have had friends and loved ones who were hurt in accidents that might have been avoided. My friend was Danny, and he was permanently disabled because he did not adequately check that the pole that he was about to climb was not rotted.

Do any of you have a friend like Danny, who was disabled or killed in a workplace accident? Send me a chat message about them.

Summary

I realize that most of you came here because it was required by your manager. You probably had better things to do, and at first you did not feel very positive about this presentation.

Please take a few moments now to answer some polling questions. This will help me in conducting such presentations in the future.

- Did you get anything out of this presentation?

- What?

- When you get back to work today, what will you say about this presentation to your coworkers?

- Have I and the other members of the group helped you in any way to increase the chances that you will come home safely tonight, and every other night as well?

Thank you very much for your time. My e-mail address is myemail@mycompany.com. I will be sending you a short evaluation sheet. Please answer the questions frankly. They are just for me and will not be shared with anyone else. And, of course, kindly contact me if you have any questions now or in the future.

Now, please disconnect from this presentation.

VIRTUAL ICEBREAKERS AND OTHER GAMES

PLEASED TO MAKE YOUR ACQUAINTANCE

Type of Activity

Icebreaker

Goal

To acquaint attendees with one another and build a warm and friendly climate.

How to Conduct

1. Ask each participant to send a chat to the group, including his name and five words or brief phrases that identify something

about him that can be a conversation starter. These may include something about where he lives (e.g., state, desert, mountains, coast, ranch), his hobbies, his pets, and other such information. Allow 5 minutes.

A sample entry is

Joel Gendelman: (1) Colorado, (2) foothills, (3) swing dancer, (4) owns two mastiffs, and (5) rides horses.

2. Direct each participant to begin chatting with another participant whose introduction she finds interesting.

3. After two or three minutes, ask participants to select another partner.

4. Do this a few more times.

5. Conduct a discussion using the following polling questions:

   ◦ Did you meet anyone interesting?

   ◦ What types of information did you find most useful (e.g., demographics, hobby, job responsibilities, or something else)?

   ◦ How well do you feel you fit into this group?

Approximate Time

No more than 10 minutes.

* * *

THE MYSTERY GUEST

Type of Activity

Icebreaker

Goal

To encourage attendees to meet as many other attendees as possible.

How to Conduct

1. Prior to the presentation, designate someone as the Mystery Guest. Do this with a pre-presentation telephone call or e-mail.

2. Arrange it so that the Mystery Guest may assume several names and direct her to change names or identities after handing out each prize.

3. Clearly indicate in your pre-presentation communications that there will be a Mystery Guest and that anyone who introduces himself to this guest will receive a prize (e.g., a $10 Amazon.com gift certificate).

4. Direct attendees to introduce themselves to as many other participants as possible, using the chat feature. Tell them that if they introduce themselves to the Mystery Guest, they will receive a prize.

5. Announce prizes as they are earned and distribute them at the end of the session.

Approximate Time

No more than 10 minutes.

* * *

BINGO HELLO

Type of Activity

Icebreaker

Goal

To encourage attendees to introduce themselves in a nonthreatening manner.

How to Conduct

1. Prepare a unique bingo card for each participant. The entries will identify personal characteristics. See below for an example of such a card.

2. Direct participants to begin chatting with other participants to determine which one fits the characteristics on their bingo card until they score a bingo. Ask the participant to write her name in the appropriate slot.

Plays tennis _____	Has grandchildren _____	Has cats _____	Has two or more dogs _____	Drives a pickup
Is wearing red _____	Flies a plane _____	Speaks more than one foreign language _____	Has red hair _____	Has brown eyes _____
Was raised abroad	Is a runner _____	Is a swimmer _____	Is a horseback rider _____	Rides a motorcycle _____
Dances regularly _____	Is an artist _____	Is a musician _____	Is a published writer _____	Lives in the city _____
Lives in the country _____	Owns a boat _____	Ice skates _____	Rollerblades _____	Rides a skateboard _____

3. Conduct a discussion using the following polling questions:

Did you find it easy to gather the information that you needed in a virtual environment?

What did you find worked?

What did you find that did not work?

Approximate Time

No more than 15 minutes.

* * *

SNAPSHOT

Type of Activity

Icebreaker

Goal

For attendees to become better acquainted with one another by being able to visualize what they look like.

How to Conduct

1. Prior to the presentation, ask each attendee to send the producer/moderator a snapshot or caricature of herself.

2. Ask the producer/moderator to create a slide or document that contains the person's name and the picture or caricature.

3. At the beginning of the presentation, conduct a short game by presenting a description of an attendee (e.g., long red hair) and asking the group to either speak out or send a chat with her name.

Approximate Time

No more than 10 minutes.

* * *

BRAINSTORMING

Type of Activity

Creative problem solving

Goal

To provide participants with practice in brainstorming creative solutions to real-world problems.

Research indicates that creativity can be cultivated using simple and practical exercises. However, the spark of innovative thinking is often dimmed by phrases such as, "We tried that before," "We have always done it this way," and the like. Use this activity to rekindle the attendees' spark of creativity.

How to Conduct

1. Read the following story.

> A man named Spencer Silver was working in the 3M research laboratories in 1970, trying to find a strong adhesive. Silver developed a new adhesive, but it was even weaker than what 3M already manufactured. It stuck to objects, but it could easily be lifted off. No one knew what to do with the stuff. Then one Sunday four years later, another 3M scientist named Arthur Fry was singing in his church's choir. He used slips of paper to keep his place in the hymnal, but they kept falling out of the book. Remembering Silver's adhesive, Fry used some to coat his slips of paper. With the weak adhesive, the markers stayed in place, yet they could be lifted

off without damaging the pages when he wanted to remove them. 3M began distributing Post-it Notes nationwide in 1980—10 years after Silver developed this weak adhesive. Today they are one of the most popular office products available.

2. Conduct a short discussion on the value of thinking outside the box and the use of brainstorming as a method of generating innovative and new ideas.

3. Post a challenge to the group, such as, suggest as many uses of plastic kitchen wrap as you can in three minutes.

4. Stress the following rules:

   ○ Attendees may not post any judgments, such as, "That's silly."

   ○ Freewheeling is welcome; the wilder the idea, the better.

   ○ Focus on quantity, not quality.

   ○ Feel free to improve or combine the ideas of others.

5. Be sure to enforce the rules.

6. Ask your producer/moderator to keep track of the responses and tally the number of original ideas.

7. Use the whiteboard feature to highlight the craziest and most far-out ideas of the group.

8. Conduct a short discussion on the following questions, using the whiteboard feature.

   ○ Did you feel that this technique was helpful in generating some unique uses of plastic kitchen wrap that you would never have considered by yourself?

   ○ Are you working on anything where you would consider using brainstorming as a technique? What is it?

   ○ What challenges do you foresee, and how can you avoid them?

Nice Idea

Use a burning match simulation to illustrate how much time attendees have left to come up with ideas. You can find such a simulation at http://www.swishzone.com/index.php?area=resources&tab=movies&do=page&action=detailed&link_id=497.

Approximate Time

10 to 15 minutes.

* * *

WHAT DO EMPLOYEES REALLY WANT?

Type of Activity

Management and supervisory skills exercise

Goal

For managers and supervisors to appreciate the motivation of their employees and how it may differ from their own.

Most new supervisors and managers assume that the things that motivate them are the same as the things that motivate their staff. Well, that isn't necessarily true. This activity drives this point home and convinces new managers and supervisors that they should constantly check their own perceptions of how their staff views things.

How to Conduct

1. Ask the attendees to rank the importance of the following in motivating employees. Use the polling feature, but do not display the results yet.

- Working conditions
- Job security
- Promotion
- High wages
- Appreciation for a job well done
- Management loyalty
- Feeling that they have a role in major decisions
- Interesting and fulfilling work
- Fair treatment
- Assistance with personal problems

2. Display the results.

3. Use the whiteboard to compare these results with those obtained by surveys of thousands of other supervisors and managers throughout the country. Those results are

    1. High wages
    2. Job security
    3. Promotion
    4. Working conditions
    5. Interesting and fulfilling work
    6. Management loyalty
    7. Fair treatment
    8. Appreciation for a job well done
    9. Assistance with personal problems
    10. Feeling that they have a role in major decisions

4. Announce that you will now compare the group's results with the rankings from surveys of the employees themselves. These are

    1. Appreciation for a job well done

    2. Feeling that they have a role in major decisions

    3. Assistance with personal problems

    4. Job security

    5. High wages

    6. Interesting and fulfilling work

    7. Promotion

    8. Management loyalty

    9. Working conditions

    10. Fair treatment

5. Conduct a short discussion on the discrepancy between what managers and supervisors feel affects employee motivation and the feelings of the employees themselves. Stress that the top three items ranked by employees are the three that are felt to be least important by their supervisors and managers. Also address the following questions:

    ○ What factors might affect this difference of opinion between managers/supervisors and their employees?

    ○ Do you think that you would find the same difference in your group, department, and company?

Approximate Time

20 minutes

* * *

RESPONDING TO OBJECTIONS

Type of Activity

Promoting interaction in sales presentations

Goal

To provide attendees with practice in responding to customer objections.

How to Conduct

1. Prepare a list of possible customer objections and assign a number to each objection.

2. If you have not already done so, prepare a list of attendees and assign a number to each attendee.

3. Ask your producer/moderator to select two numbers: one to identify the objection, and the other to identify the participant who will respond to the objection.

4. Read the objection aloud and ask the attendee to respond spontaneously to the objection verbally.

5. Open up the objection to the rest of the group and ask attendees to throw out a few other ideas. Give them no more than 30 seconds to respond.

6. Ask the initial responder which of these ideas she would like to incorporate in her response.

7. Repeat Steps 3 through 6 for the remainder of the "critical" objections related to your new product that customers may voice.

8. Wrap up this activity with a short discussion of the most important objections that the group needs to rehearse responding to.

9. Break attendees into pairs and ask each pair to arrange a telephone
   call with each other where they can rehearse responding to these
   objections.

Nice Idea

Use a burning match simulation to illustrate how much time attendees
have left to respond to the objection. You can find such a simulation
at http://www.swishzone.com/index.php?area=resources&tab=movies
&do=page&action=detailed&link_id=497.

Approximate Time

15 to 20 minutes.

* * *

GREAT IDEAS

Type of Activity

Decision making

Goal

To generate a multitude of ideas related to dealing with an issue or to
solving a problem. This technique prevents a few vocal attendees from
dominating a discussion and encourages quieter members of the audience to participate in the discussion.

How to Conduct

1. Ask a question, such as, how can we get more large corporate
   accounts involved in our product development process?

2. Ask each attendee to send the producer/moderator at least three ideas, using the chat feature. Give participants two minutes to respond.

3. Work with the producer/moderator to select what you feel are the 20 most valuable suggestions.

4. Conduct a poll to allow the group to select its favorite three suggestions. Hide the results until the end of the poll.

5. Display the results of the poll. Thank attendees for their help. Indicate that you will be sharing these suggestions with management.

Nice Idea

Use a burning match simulation to illustrate how much time attendees have left to respond to the poll. You can find such a simulation at http://www.swishzone.com/index.php?area=resources&tab=movies &do=page&action=detailed&link_id=497.

Approximate Time

15 to 20 minutes.

BIBLIOGRAPHY

Bartlett, John. *Bartlett's Familiar Quotations: A Collection of Passages, Phrases, and Proverbs Traced to Their Sources in Ancient and Modern Literature*, 17th ed. New York: Bartleby, 2009.

Block, Arthur. *Murphy's Law*, 26th ed. Berkeley, Calif.: Berkeley Publishing Group, 2003.

Einstein, Albert. "Imagination Quotes." http://www.wisdomquotes.com/cat_imagination.html; accessed October 15, 2009.

Frost & Sullivan. *Measuring the True Benefits of Web Collaboration: Demystifying the Productivity Paradox*. White paper sponsored by WebEx Communications, October 2005.

Holmes, Oliver W. *Vaughan College Magazine* 1, no. 1 (2004– 2005).

Litera.uk.com. "Mark Hamilton." http://www.litera.co.uk/author/mark_hamilton/; accessed October 15, 2009.

Neilssen, A., and A. Greenbert. *The Evolving Role of Web Seminars and On-line Events in the Marketing Mix: Applications & Results from a Sales and Marketing Perspective*. Study conducted by Wainhouse Research and sponsored by WebEx Communications, October 2008.

Sandburg, Carl. *The Complete Poems of Carl Sandburg*. Orlando, Fla.: Harcourt, Inc., 1970.

Shakespeare, William. *As You Like It*. New York: Washington Square Press, 1997.

Thiagarajan, Sivasailam. *Thiagi's Interactive Lectures*. Alexandria, Va.: American Society for Training and Development, 2005.

Twain, Mark. Thinkexist.com. http://thinkexist.com/quotation/i_didn-t_have_time_to_write_a_short_letter-so_i/338386.html; accessed October 15, 2009.

ADDITIONAL RESOURCES

Accelerating the Sale: How WebTouch Selling Enhances Traditional Face-to-Face Selling. White paper published by Sales Benchmark Index.

Althaus, S. "Computer-Mediated Communication in the University Classroom: An Experiment with On-Line Discussions." *Communication Education* 46 (1997), pp. 158–174.

Anderson, M. "Using Computer Conferencing and Electronic Mail to Facilitate Group Projects." *Journal of Educational Technology Systems* 24, no. 2 (1996), pp. 113–118.

Anderson, T., L. Rourke, D. R. Garrison, and W. Archer. "Assessing Teaching Presence in a Computer Conferencing Environment." *Journal of Asynchronous Learning Networks* 5, no. 2 (2001).

Aviv, R., and G. Golan. "Pedagogical Communication Patterns in Collaborative Telelearning." *Journal of Educational Technology Systems* 26, no. 3 (1998), pp. 201–208.

Backroad Connections Pty Ltd. *Effective Online Facilitation*, Version 2.00. Australian Flexible Learning Framework Quick Guides series, Australian National Training Authority, 2002.

Beaudoin, M. F. "Learning or Lurking? Tracking the 'Invisible' Online Student." *The Internet and Higher Education* 5 (2002), pp. 147–155.

Beise, C. M., F. Niederman, and P. M. Beranek. "Group Facilitation in a Networked World." *Group Facilitation* 1 (1999), pp. 33–44.

Berge, Z. L. "Electronic Discussion Groups." *Communication Education* 43, no. 2 (1994), pp. 102–111.

Berge, Z. L. "Facilitating Computer Conferencing: Recommendations from the Field." *Educational Technology* 35, no. 1 (1995), pp. 22–30.

Berge, Z. L., and M. P. Collins, eds. *Computer Mediated Communication and the Online Classroom.* 3 vols. Cresskill, N.J.: Hampton Press, 1995.

Berge, Z. L., and M. P. Collins, eds. *Computer-Mediated Communication and the Online Classroom: Distance Education.* Cresskill, N.J.: Hampton Press, 1995.

Beyond Bullet Points. http://www.beyondbulletpoints.com/; accessed October 15, 2009.

Bonwell, C. C., and J. A. Eison. *Active Learning: Creating Excitement in the Classroom.* ASHE-ERIC Higher Education Report No. 1. Washington, D.C.: George Washington University, School of Education and Human Development, 1991.

Brookfield, S. D., and S. Preskill. *Discussion as a Way of Teaching.* San Francisco: Jossey-Bass, 1997.

Brouwer, P. "Hold On a Minute Here: What Happened to Critical Thinking in the Information Age?" *Journal of Educational Technology Systems* 25, no. 2 (1996), pp. 189–197.

Carter, V., and A. Deden. "Using Technology to Enhance Student Skills." In *New Directions for Higher Education,* edited by E. Jones. San Francisco: Jossey-Bass, 1996, pp. 81–92.

Clark, R., and Ann Kwin. *The New Virtual Classroom.* San Francisco: John Wiley & Sons, 2007.

Collins, Mauri. *Facilitating Interaction in Computer Mediated Online Presentations.* Background paper presented at the FSU/AECT Distance Education Conference, Tallahassee, Florida, June 1996.

Collison, G., B. Elbaum, S. Haavind, and R. Tinker. *Facilitating Online Learning: Effective Strategies for Moderators.* Madison, Wis.: Atwood Publishing, 2000.

CXO Media. *Collaborative Efforts: Survey Reveals Clear Business Acceleration Using On-Demand Collaboration Technology.* White paper sponsored by WebEx Communications.

Dennis, A. R., and J. S. Valacich. "Electronic Brainstorming: Illusions and Patterns of Productivity." *Information Systems Research* 10 (1999), pp. 375–377.

Dickson, G. W., J. L. Partridge, M. Limayem, and G. L. Desanctis. "Facilitating Computer-Supported Meetings: A Cumulative Analysis in a Multiple-Criteria Task Environment." *Group Decision and Negotiation* 5 (1996), pp. 51–72.

evolvingWe. "10 Tips for Running Live Virtual Presentations." http://evolvingwe.com/business/10-tips-for-running-live-virtual-presentations; accessed October 15, 2009.

Ezine. "How to Develop a Winning Virtual Presentation." http://ezinearticles.com/?How-to-Develop-a-Winning-Virtual-Presentation&id=2288818; accessed October 15, 2009.

Furst, S., R. Blackburn, and B. Rosen. "Virtual Team Effectiveness: A Proposed Research Agenda." *Information Systems Journal* 9 (1999), pp. 249–269.

Gayeski, D. M. *Designing and Managing Computer Mediated Learning: An Interactive Toolkit*, 3rd ed. Ithaca, N.Y.: OmniCom Associates, 1997.

Gendelman, J. "Energizing Virtual Instruction." *Learning Circuits*, November 2008.

Gendelman, J. "Energizing Virtual Meetings." *Intercom* 56, no. 2 (2009), pp. 28–29.

Gorsky, P., and A. Caspi. "Dialogue: A Theoretical Framework for Distance Education Instructional Systems." *British Journal of Educational Technology* 36, no. 2 (2005), pp. 137–144.

Griffith, T. L., M. A. Fuller, and G. B. Northcraft. "Facilitator Influence in Group Support Systems: Intended and Unintended Effects." *Information Systems Research* 9 (1998), pp. 20–36.

Growing Your Business through Real-Time Collaboration: An Introduction to Web Meeting Applications. White paper published by WebEx Communications.

Gschwandtner, G. *How Web Conferencing Accelerated Your Sales Process: A Guide for Making Your Customer Relationships More Profitable.* White paper sponsored by WebEx Communications.

Hanna, Donald E., M. Glowacki-Dudka, and S. Conceicao-Runlee. *147 Practical Tips for Teaching Online Groups: Essentials of Web-Based Education.* Overland Park, Kans.: Atwood Publishing, 2000.

Harasim, L., R. Starr, L. Teles, and M. Turoff, eds. *Learning Networks: A Field Guide to Teaching and Learning Online.* Cambridge, Mass.: MIT Press, 1995.

Hayne, S. C. "The Facilitator's Perspective on Meetings and Implications for Group Support System Design." *Database for Advances in Information Systems* 30 (1999), pp. 72–89.

Hewitt, J. "How Habitual Online Practices Affect the Development of Asynchronous Discussion Threads." *Journal of Educational Computing Research* 28, no. 1 (2003), pp. 31–45.

Hewitt, J. "Toward an Understanding of How Threads Die in Asynchronous Computer Conferences." *Journal of the Learning Sciences* 14, no. 4 (2005), pp. 567–589.

Howard, Chris. *Virtual Classroom Technology: Hitachi Data Systems Establishes Implementation Framework for Virtual Instructor-Led Training Programs.* Case study by Bersin & Associates, 2006.

Jeong, A. "The Combined Effects of Response Time and Message Content on Growth Patterns of Discussion Threads in Computer-Supported

Collaborative Argumentation." *Journal of Distance Education* 19, no. 1 (2004), pp. 36–53.

Ko, Susan, and Steve Rossen. *Teaching Online: A Practical Guide.* Boston: Houghton Mifflin, 2001.

Kock, N. "Benefits for Virtual Organizations from Distributed Groups." *Communications of the ACM* 43 (2000), pp. 107–112.

Mahowald, Robert. 2000. *Using Web Conferencing to Ensure Successful Enterprise Application Deployment. Adapted from Worldwide Conferencing Applications 2005–2009 Forecast: A First Look at 2004 Performance and Key Trends,* Document # 33150.

Mayadas, F., J. Bourne, and J. Moore. "Introduction." In *Elements of Quality Online Education,* edited by J. Bourne and J. Moore. Needham, Mass.: Sloan Consortium, 2002.

Mazzolini, M., and S. Maddison. "Sage, Guide or Ghost? The Effect of Instructor Intervention on Student Participation in Online Discussion Forums." *Computers and Education* 40 (2003), pp. 237–253.

McNeil, D. P. "Computer Conferencing: The Causes for Delay." In *Empowering Networks: Computer Conferencing in Education,* edited by M. D. Waggoner. Englewood Cliffs, N.J.: Educational Technology Publications, 1992.

Miranda, S. M., and R. P. Bostrom. "Meeting Facilitation: Process versus Content Interventions." *Journal of Management Information Systems* 15 (1999), pp. 89–114.

Mittleman, D. D., R. O. Briggs, and J. F. Nunamaker. "Best Practices in Facilitating Virtual Meetings: Some Notes from Initial Experience." *Group Facilitation* 2 (2000), pp. 5–14.

Molay, Ken. *Best Practices for Webinars. Increasing Attendance, Engaging Your Audience, and Successfully Advancing Your Business Goals.* White paper published by Adobe Inc., 2009.

The New Competitive Advantage: Web Collaboration Reaches the Tipping Point. Technology brief published by WebEx Communications.

Niederman, F., C. M. Beise, and P. M. Beranek. "Issues and Concerns about Computer-Supported Meetings: The Facilitator's Perspective." *MIS Quarterly* 20 (1996), pp. 1–22.

Nilssen, A., and A. Davis. *Unearthing the True Value of Web Seminars and On-line Events.* Study conducted by Wainhouse Research and sponsored by WebEx Communications, September 2005.

Nonnecke, B., and J. Preece. "Why Lurkers Lurk." *AMCIS Conference, Boston,* June 2001.

Oblinger, D., and K. Hafner. "Transforming the Academy." In *The Future Compatible Campus.* Boston: Anker Publishing Co., 1998, pp. 3–23.

Odin, Jaishree K. "Teaching and Learning Activities in the Online Classroom: A Constructivist Perspective." In *World Conference on Educational Multimedia, Hypermedia, and Telecommunications, Proceedings.* Association for the Advancement of Computing in Education, Denver, Col., 2002.

Online Marketing Events: Best Practices for Optimizing ROI with WebEx Event Center. White paper published by WebEx Communications, 2005.

Palloff, Rena M., and Keith Pratt. *Building Learning Communities in Cyberspace: Effective Strategies for the Online Classroom.* San Francisco: Jossey-Bass, 1999.

Phillips, L. D., and M. C. Phillips. "Facilitated Work Groups: Theory and Practice. *Journal of the Operational Research Society* 44 (1993), pp. 533–549.

Plummer, Tim. *Acrobat Connect Professional Essential Training.* CD-ROM. Lynda.com, 2007.

Powers, S., and J. Mitchell. *Student Perceptions and Performance in the Virtual Classroom Environment.* University of Hawaii-Minoa, ERIC Document Reproduction Service No. ED 409 005, 1997.

Presentation Zen. http://www.presentationzen.com/; accessed October 15, 2009.

Qureshi, S., and D. Vogel. "Adaptiveness in Virtual Teams: Organizational Challenges and Research Directions." *Group Decision and Negotiation* 10 (2001), pp. 27–46.

Reach the World. Brochure published by WebEx Communications, 2005.

Sackville, A. "Designing for Interaction." In *Proceedings of the Third International Conference, Networked Learning,* Sheffield University, 2002, pp. 534–541.

Sackville, A., and M. Schofield. "A Framework for the Evaluation of Networked Learning and the Implications of Evaluative Research for the Process of Re-design." In *Proceedings of the Fourth International Conference, Networked Learning,* Sheffield University, 2004.

Salida, A. *Living Large: Small Companies Yield Big Results with Web Collaboration.* White paper by Larstan Business Reports, Inc., 2007.

Salmon, G. *E-tivities: The Key to Active Online Learning.* London: Kogan Page Limited, 2002.

Sawyer, J. "Interweaving Face-to-Face Student Contact with an On-Line Class Presentation Format." ERIC Document Reproduction Services, No. ED 413 893, 1997.

Schilhl, R. J. *"Redefining Residency, Delivery Systems and Pedagogy for Doctoral Distance Education in Communication Studies via Internet."* Presented at the 87th Annual Meeting of the Eastern Communication Association, New York City, April 25–28, 1996.

Schofield, M., A. Sackville, and J. Davey. "Designing for Unique Online Learning Contexts." In *Managing Learning in Virtual Settings*, edited by A. D. de Figueiredo and A. P. Afonso. Hershey Pa.: Information Science Publishing, 2006.

Shank, P. *Making Sense of Online Learning.* San Francisco: Pfeiffer, 2004.

Starr, R. *The Virtual Classroom: Learning without Limits via Computer Networks.* Norwood, N.J.: Ablex, 2004.

Stevenson, Nancy. *WebEx for Dummies.* Hoboken, N.J.: Wiley, 2005.

Swan, K. "Building Learning Communities in Online Courses: The Importance of Interaction." *Education, Communication and Information* 2, no. 1 (2002), pp. 23–49.

Taking Remote Support to the Next Level. White paper published by Service Excellence Research Group, 2005.

Tan, B. C., K. Wei, and J. L. Partridge. "Effects of Facilitation and Leadership on Meeting Outcomes in a Group Support System Environment." *European Journal of Information Systems* 8 (1999), pp. 233–246.

Turoff, M., S. R. Hiltz, A. Baghat, and A. Rana. "Distributed Group Support Systems." *MIS Quarterly* 17 (1993), pp. 399–417.

Warkentin, M. E., L. Sayeed, and R. Hightower. "Virtual Teams versus Face-to-Face Teams: An Exploratory Study of a Web-Based Conference System." *Decision Sciences* 28 (1997), pp. 975–996.

Web Conferencing Community Forum, http://www.wcc-forum.com.

White, Ken, and Bob Weight. *The Online Teaching Guide: A Handbook of Attitudes, Strategies, and Techniques for the Virtual Classroom.* Boston: Allyn & Bacon, 2000.

Wright, B. E., and J. Rohrbaugh. "Evaluating the Strengths and Weaknesses of Group Decision Making Processes: A Competing Values Approach." *Group Facilitation* 1 (1999), pp. 5–13.

INDEX

ABOUT THE AUTHOR

Dr. Joel Gendelman conducts workshops and provides on-site and virtual consulting to assist organizations in conducting great virtual presentations (http://www.greatvirtualpresentations.com). As president and founder of Future Technologies Inc., he has more than 25 years of experience in developing activity-rich corporate presentations and communications for companies that include Lockheed Martin, Microsoft, Nissan, Lucent Technologies, Hewlett-Packard, Amgen, and Genentech (http://www.fttraining.com).

This is Joel's third book. He has also written two books to help new consultants build a successful consulting firm and experienced consultants grow their firm (http://www.consulting-mentor.com).

In addition to his books, Joel has published more than 26 articles. He has won several awards in the areas of communications, training, and performance improvement and is a frequent speaker at international conferences and corporate events. Joel holds both a Master's and a Doctorate in Educational Technology from the Catholic University of America.